Echoes From Other Worlds

An Anthology of Fiction in Two Parts

By
Wendy Easterling, Scott Goodrich, Kenneth King,
Bobby Matherne, Shana L. Martin, Keith McGraw,
Sharon Robb-Chism, Stephen Sanders,
Pamala A. Williams and Kittye Williams

Illustrations by
Sharon Robb-Chism and Rod Lindsey

Cover Art by
Rod Lindsey, Sharon Robb-Chism,
and Stephen Sanders

Blackbead Books
ISBN: 978-0-578-04588-7
www.blackbead-jewelry.com

To the writer who has inspired each of us the most –
Whoever that may be.

Let us be silent for a little while;
Let us be still and listen. We may hear
Echoes from other worlds not far a way.

An Excerpt from "It May Be"
By Ella Wheeler Wilcox,
1859 - 1919

Last year, we brought you Raising Black Flags as our first attempt at an anthology of unpublished, first time poets. It has been a great success, scoring excellent reviews and introducing the world to some excellent poetry. The book has appeared at the Texas Renaissance Festival, the Port Washington Pirate Festival, Pyrate Days on the Queen Mary, Scarlet's Mid-Winter Renaissance Faire, and Middlefaire, among other festivals, faires, and dozens of booksellers' websites. Poems from the book have been recited all over the country (and as far away as London, England!)

This year, we wanted to extend our reach so we included short stories. We also wanted to show you another side of our imaginations so we've added science fiction and fantasy pieces. We are very proud of this book and we hope that you enjoy every poem, every short story and every image created by the incredible contributors.

As we considered the title for this book, a story about Raising Black Flags kept coming back to us. One of our readers told us about a visit from her daughter's family over the summer. The daughter's son, who had never been a big fan of poetry, found his grandmother's copy of our book.

During the week, he read Raising Black Flags from cover to cover. His grandmother said that she would walk in on him and he would be sitting quietly and reading the poems about sea battles, cursed pirate ships, and love, life and death at sea.

After her grandson and his family left to go home, during the long trip in the car, the boy's mother called the grandmother. She had to relate that the boy was sitting in the backseat of the family car, reciting one of the poems from the book – which he had memorized.

In the first place, everyone involved in Black Flags was incredibly moved by the thought that something we had created had reached a young man to the extent that he memorized a portion of it. It is an incredible feeling, one that gives us all goose bumps to this day.

But even more amazing, is the image of that young man, sitting and reading our book, totally engrossed in the tales we told and the images we created. That moment is what writers dream about – a reader truly appreciating your effort and being enchanted by the magic you hoped you had spun.

It was this image that made me think of Ella Wheeler Wilcox's incredible poem, "It May Be," a small portion of which is set out above. Ms. Wilcox's name may not be familiar to you but her poetry most likely is. While not a famous or celebrated name, her poetry has touched the lives of millions of people. She wrote for the common man and has been called "a popular poet rather than a literary poet." She published over twenty volumes of poetry but the one you will remember is "Solitude", which begins: "Laugh and the world laughs with you, Weep, and you weep alone . . ." To read more about her, or her works, search for the Ella Wheeler Wilcox Society on the World Wide Web.

Ms. Wheeler's "It May Be" rhymes of other worlds, other dimensions, and other people, which make our world a "zone of wonder." She suggests that these worlds and the people that inhabit them may just be awaiting our call to join us in the "rarefied regions" in which we all dwell. One interpretation of this poem is that she is talking about characters in the tales and poems and songs of those that write and sing. All one must do is open a book to call on these "beings" and there you may join them in that "zone of wonder."

What we hope to provide for you in Echoes From Other Worlds is a portal to one of the places Ms. Wheeler might have been writing about and to a whole legion of "curious people and races, Folk of the fourth dimension, folk of the vast star spaces." Come and sit still with us and read these new tales of pirates, aliens, Death, demons, dragons, and everything in between!

"Thanks, mates!"

I wish to sincerely thank everyone who had a role in creating and producing this book. Thanks to all of the writers, poets and artists who contributed their work for Echoes and special thanks to the people who proofread, made suggestions, and helped with the artwork. Extra special thanks go out to Bobby Matherne for not only reading every work but for "editing the editor." And, of course, thank you and all my love to Melody, "the captain's Captain."

TABLE OF CONTENTS

List of Illustrations

Biographies of the Authors and Poets

WENDY EASTERLING began writing poetry, lyrics and short stories as soon as she figured out that she could say whatever she wanted, just so long as it either rhymed or had quotation marks... and she's been raising eyebrows ever since. While lately residing in Edmond, OK, Wendy and her daughter travel frequently to attend Renaissance Festivals and SciFi conventions, where they find inspiration for their various writing projects.

SCOTT GOODRICH is a bit of a Jack of All Trades. An artist, thinker, fabricationist, and would be removal expert, all rolled in with a whole bunch of other stuff to make a well rounded individual. He has lived mostly in the United States somewhere, being an army brat, with a small stint in Germany. He was not always the most ideological, or coordinated individual now before you. Most of his inspirations come from dreams and short brainstorms that appear out of nowhere or from playing some RPG game with friends. Today, living with his fantastic wife Colleen, if he is not sleeping he is working hard at a new idea in the garage or some other project that has been piling up, after a hard day of graphic designing for a local trade show company in Dallas Texas.

KENNETH KING is a graduate of the University of Texas with a degree in Film, Television, and Radio, Ken has spent the better part of his life on the move. An Army brat, he has traveled all over the continental United States and Europe. He also spent a year living in Japan teaching English. His camera has been his "eye to the world" since he was in high school but his interest in pirates and digital art has come later in life. Recently, Ken published a book of photography entitled The Stone Garden which is available through Blackbead Books..

ROD LINDSEY was born in Dallas, Texas, in 1966 – one day after his life long hero, Walt Disney, died. From a very early age, he knew that he wanted to draw cartoons and fantasy art. But, after being told to "grow up" by some of his teachers, he spent the better part of his life following other career paths to fee his two daughters, Raechel and Ashleigh. But he continued to draw for his own enjoyment. In 2002, he met and married Kristina Hunt and she became his biggest fan. With her support, he is taking he first steps to finally living his dream! Most recently, he's created a logo for a local band and he's learning to use more and more software to expand his art skills.

BOBBY MATHERNE is a writer, poet, novelist, photographer, cartoonist, publisher, physicist, psychotherapist, computer scientist, philosopher, and researcher into the evolution of consciousness. He has published in several scientific journals, and his recently published books are The SPIZZNET FILE - An Adventure in Inter-species Communication (2000), A Reader's Journal - Journeys into Understanding (1997), Rainbows and Shadows (1995), Flowers of Shanidar (1991) and Freedom on the Half Shell (1990). Since 2000, he has been writing primarily on the Internet at www.doyletics.com. On a clear day, he can be found leaning on the cyber-fence talking to friends around the world about doyletics, a new science of understanding human processes that he has recently founded and for which he is the Principal Researcher.

SHANA L. MARTIN is a poet, a dancer, a writer of tales, a singer, and a lover of life. She hails from Largo, Florida; a community next door to Tampa Bay. Shana believes that her writing ability is a gift from God. She is inspired by many different places, people and things; which is why in most cases she puts the name of what inspires the work at the end of the piece – a "whispered" "thank you" for the unique creative spark that they gave her. Writing is her way of expressing those feelings and thoughts that might otherwise might go unsaid.

KEITH MCGRAW's previous articles have been internationally published in professional security and counter-terrorism journals. He has multiple fiction projects in the works (read "half written and now on-hold pending time and inspiration"), most of which deal with either military or criminal subject matter. His background in the United States Marine Corps and as a Private Investigator provide obvious insight as to why that is. Though he has spent time in Japan, Korea, China, Phillipines, Hawaii, Poland, Belarus, Mexico, California, and other foreign countries, Keith is Texan to the bone. He is currently in active service with the Texas State Guard Maritime Regiment. Keith relates he was inspired to write the poem "Death or Glory" when he saw a Military History magazine cover with Napoleonic era cavalrymen on it.

SHARON ROBB-CHISM was always told by her parents she had an overactive imagination. She majored in art, writing only for her own entertainment. Later in life she gave a short-story to a friend to read, who convinced her to join a writer's group. Sharon joined the Barn Owls Writer's Group and has enjoyed writing everything from fantasy to mystery novels. She also enjoys dressing up as a pirate as part of the Tales of the Seven Seas reenactment group. Apparently, Sharon still has an overactive imagination. She lives Southern Oregon with her husband, Robert, and five spoiled cats.

STEPHEN SANDERS has been writing since he was ten – his first short story was for his mother and was about a boy who winds up in a tiger pit . . . Since then, he's written and lived in Texas, Louisiana, Virginia, Germany, and Washington, DC. These days, his tales are mostly about pirates but what he wants to do more than anything is bring back the voice and style of "adventure poetry" as written by the likes of Kipling and Tennyson and Poe. He currently lives in Fort Worth, TX, with his lovely wife, Melody, and their two cats. Stephen's poetry has won numerous awards, been published in magazines and books, and is the source of infinite joy to his mother!

KITTYE WILLIAMS is a native of Vinita, Oklahoma, Kittye is the creator, owner, and manager of The Ladies of the Salty Kiss (see their website at www.theladiesofthesaltykiss.com). Kittye comes from a musical background, having performed in a variety of musical ensembles and vocal choirs throughout her school years. Hooked after attending her first renaissance faire, she became a "professional" actress nine years ago. She enjoys making people laugh and tends to be the troupe's practical joker. When not performing with her troupe, she can be found pursuing the other love of her life, nursing as a Registered Nurse.

PAMALA A. WILLIAMS has been writing since she could hold a pencil. She has written numerous poems, short stories and is currently working on a book series. She has been published in magazines and a book anthology. She is inspired by what she sees, what she hears, and what she dreams.

Tales From The Sea

It's In Me Blood

I remember . . .
The pub were crowded the night we met,
Ol' Benny Hawkins and me.
The crew were rowdy – we sailed the next day –
And the rum were flowin' quite free!
I sat and watched Ben drink all night
And drunker and drunker he became.
Sailin' together, we were soon fast mates,
And I found Ben's nights were all the same.
I'd seen the drink kill a man before,
And I hated to watch it take Ol' Ben down,
So I waited for a night when he weren't so in his cups
And there weren't any other crewmen hangin' 'roun'.
Hearin' me out, he answered,
"I know I should stop drinkin', I should!
But I fear it's in me blood, boy," he said,
"The Devil's thirst, aye! It's in me blood."

I remember . . .
The deck were hot as we stood to,
Me and the rest of the men,
To watch Ol' Benny take a lashing,
For he had been fightin' again.
He'd pulled a knife in the fo'c'sle,
Near takin' another man's eye,
The 'master had warned him 'bout fightin',
So they beat Ben till he come near to die.
Later I tended the cat's scratches
With bits o'sail covered with lard,
And I asked him, "Why must ye be a brawler
When it makes your life so hard?"
Grittin' his teeth, he answered,
"I'd stop me fightin' if only I could!
But I fear it's in me blood, boy," he said,
"The red rage, aye! It's in me blood."

5

I remember . . .
The ship were burnin' like Hades
As we fought to take a new prize,
And that was the day Ol'Ben become a hero;
I saw it with me own two eyes.
We were havin' the worst of the battle
When Ol'Ben charged the enemy crew!
He rallied our men and he saved us . . .
But he paid the Devil his due.
I knelt by Ol' Ben at the last moment,
As the light slowly slipped from his eyes,
And I asked him, "Why did you do it?"
And the answer came as a surprise:
"You men, you're all like me family,
"And it's me home, this ol' hunk of wood,
And I guess it's in me blood, boy," he said,
"A pirate's life, aye! It's in me blood!"

Stephen Sanders
©2009

The Horses Of Neptune

It has always held a fascination for me.
Wondering if they will ever break free,
The horses of the sea…

With their white frothy manes;
He holds tight to their reigns,
So that none brake the chains!

Sitting atop his chariot, "wave."
Those magnificent beasts are no less a slave.
Freedom is what they all want and crave.

Triton raised high in victorious hand,
He forces the score toward land.
A sight that is most grand!

Mighty is "wave's" roar,
As it thunders to shore.
Then with a crash is seen no more!

Shana L. Martin
©2008
Inspired By: God & Siren

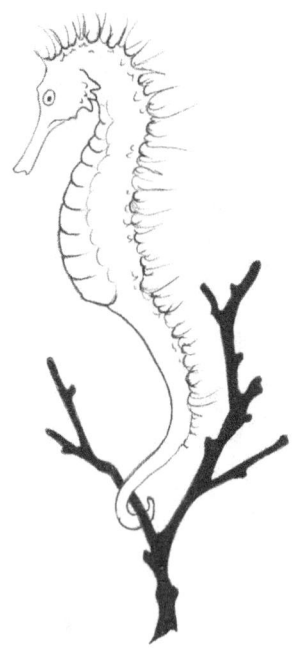

The Kracken

I think I'll spend the time I have left
     Floating among the brine and bracken
Thinking of the beauty and the horror
     Of the creature they call the Kracken

The Kracken, now, can colour change
     From grey to black to pink
And hides along the ocean floor
     Where ships are sure to sink

Its skin is smooth as smooth can be
     Its eyes as black as night
Its tentacles, now, they're something else
     They are an awesome sight

The Kracken cares not for calm or storm
     It'll strike at any hour
Day or night, it matters not
     Its fierceness is its power

It rises up from beneath the sea
     It hardly makes a sound
As it claims the ship and all on board
     Its tentacles wrap around

It crushes with its mighty strength
     And pulls the ship asunder
And men, they cry, and men, they die
     As the Kracken pulls us under

My lungs are almost empty now
     And I, well I can't swim
I curse the day I signed aboard
     This ship on just a whim

But don't mourn for me, my death today
    Aboard this cursed boat
I'm just a swabby dressed in rags
    Not in a captain's coat

I have no buttons made of brass
    No fancy frills or frapter
It is the captain, after all,
    That the Kracken is most after

Pamala A. Williams
©2009

Treasured Melody

Climbing out on the quarterdeck,
I'd spent the night tallying gold.
We'd taken a brig off Maracaibo
And her treasure now decorates our hold.

The sun's just topping the horizon,
The color of burnished copper in the air,
In my mind, I immediately see your visage,
'Cause the whole sky is the color of your hair.

Last night, I logged pearls set among rubies
And jade nuggets of various size,
But your smile makes the pearls look washed out
And the jade can't compare with your eyes.

We've taken nutmeg and pepper and sugar
But your love is all the spice I'll ever need.
We've captured silks that I can't wait to strip off you,
So I order on more canvas for more speed.

The ship leaps forward like a dolphin;
I know I need to get back below.
But counting gold now just seems like drudgery
And I still have such a long way to go.

In the distance, I can make out our headland.
If not the inventory, the journey is almost through;
And I smile because there can be no greater treasure
Than another day living and loving with you.

Stephen Sanders
©2009

Xavier Quinn

He seems no higher than a grown man's shin
And with malicious grin, he has great pride in…
 Tracking down those who pillage, plunder, and relish in sin!
Chances are slim, you'd escape from him!

East India Company's best man.
Some say he's more like the devil's own right hand.
 The Isles of Caiman to the ports of Japan,
He is known by every pirate and courtesan!

 A seemingly decent gent, who's speech is most eloquent .
'Tis hard to believe he is so hell bent,
But one look, and it becomes quite evident.
That he desires to rid the world of every malcontent!

 Known to bring down men twice his size, with the blaze of Hades in his eyes.
When he does "deal" with those he despise, it begins to crystallize.
 One can agree to "compromise" or meet with his own demise!
A word of warning to the wise… Xavier Quinn is "evil" in disguise!

Shana L. Martin
©2008
Inspired by God and Singer, Songwriter
and Actor Paul Williams

The Surgeon's Mate
© 2009 Kittye Williams

The sea stretched out before me, a sheet of green glass as far as the eyes could see. The ship was anchored off the coast a ways, secured for the night with but a handful to stand watch. The bosun's tin whistle lofted a haunting melody to the stars that wheeled over head. The carpenter sat sharpening his tools by lantern light. The cabin boy lay curled up in a coil of rope; eyes shut fast, a smile lighting his innocent features as he dreamt of more pleasurable things. And me, the surgeon's mate, sat with my feet dangling out over the side, my head resting 'gainst a well worn upright. My mind played over the months since I went to sea - how far I'd come from fair Eriu's shore and those I'd loved best.

I wondered what had become of those people I'd known all my life - would Mrs. Haggerty still be sitting on her porch, gossiping with whomever happened by? Would she even notice I was there no longer? Or did her tales have me kidnapped by sidhe and stolen underground? Of those who knew what I'd done, had any told where I'd gone? Would any care even if my conspirators had told?

And Seamus, called Mac Ruid, would he still be sailing out each morning to haul in what meager catch he could? Or had time finally taken it's toll and crippled him so he could no longer leave the shore? A kindly old salt that one had always been to me - tirelessly answering my never ending questions about the sea and her moods.

Would me mum have hurried up to the big house, asking His Lordship to send out searchers for me? Or did she sit quietly by the fire of an eve and curse me as she did my Da, who had been taken so long ago fighting 'gainst the King's men? Or had she simply forgotten me, saying "Well done with bad seed?" Sure and I was a disappointment to both my parents for different reasons. My siblings, a more noisy and rowdy bunch sure as never breathed the breath of life; always fighting amongst themselves but let any single one out - that unlucky sot had the whole gang facing him down! Aye, family may fight amongst themselves but blood will out and you pick on the one, you have the entire lot to fight.

12

Alas my sweet sloe-eyed love, my mind wandered on to a topic most painful; my thoughts turn ceaselessly to thee. Time has not erased your memory from my mind. Your voice whispers to me across the miles from your resting place to mine, even now. Tis on nights such as these; when the waves are gently lapping and the queer light dances cross the waves, your voice once more I hear, falling softly upon my ear. It's lilt and measure I know well for sure I've loved them all the days of my life. Twas cruel the way we parted, harsh words we passed back and forth; to young and pig headed to understand what it was we were truly saying. Angry with each other for the lots life had cast for us but to proud to admit such to the other.

My musings paused, interrupted by the sight and sound of a group of dolphins playing with each other in the not quite dark of this tropic place. Their laughter comes clearly to me and I find myself smiling in spite of my maudlin mood. How can one not laugh when faced with clowns such as these, whose perpetual grins have been frozen for all to see? A smaller one, braver than the rest, ventures near the ship, it's bright eye turned up towards me. He too is curious and does not quite fit in with his family. I lean forward to look closer at my strange companion and soon find myself telling my tale to this friend who is not a friend.

Time passed without my knowing. So wrapped up in spilling my woe I never heard the footfalls behind me. How long my listener stood quietly by, hearing my private words, I'll never know. Twas my newly found friend who did give the intruder away. With a chuck-chuck and flip of his tail, my friend was gone - racing away to do the things dolphins do. My head turned to the side, eyes widening with fright as they beheld the officer of the day standing not three paces behind me. Quick as you please, I'm up and on my feet, tugging my forelock in respect as my heart tries to leave my breast. How much had he heard? How much did he know? Would he inform the captain and have me set ashore? I daren't look up; afraid of the answer I'd see on his face. Silently I stood, my heart in my throat awaiting judgment.

He cleared his throat then cleared it again; I risked a peek up at him. The lieutenant shifted from foot-to-foot, he looked at me then out to sea as if to follow the dolphin's course. When he looked back at me, his voice he finally found.

13

"Surgeon's mate, pray, inform me of this tale I heard you tell yon fish. Tis a wild, unlikely story I do say; and perhaps twas my misunderstanding of your words. But tell me now, was that just a tale you crafted to keep yourself awake at your post?" He paused and looked directly into my upturned eyes.

In that moment, I found a kindly face before me - one willing to keep my secret … at least for now.

Dad, Ye Be Me Favorite Pirate

Dad, ye be me favorite pirate:
Ye taught me all I need to know,
From how to keep me cutlass clean
To where the Trade Winds blow.

You showed me how to tie me kerchief
So that it stays upon me head,
And you taught me how to use a knife
To pick the weevils from me bread.

You schooled me in me navigatin',
How to guide me ship by a star,
Ye taught me how to talk like a pirate:
When it's really correct to say "arrrr!"

Dad, ye be me favorite pirate,
And there's only one thing more to say:
Not only do I thank ye with all of me heart
But I'll join your crew any day!

Stephen Sanders
©2008

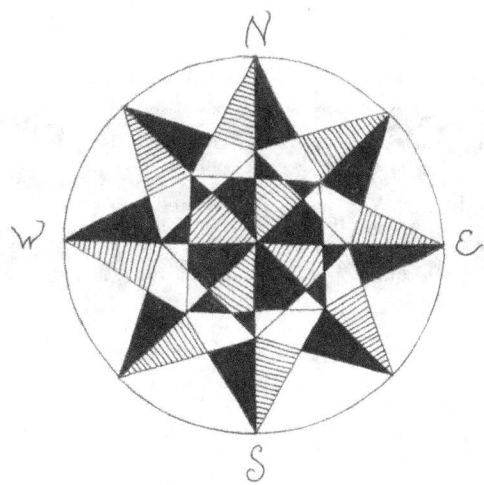

Legend Of The Compass Rose

She was beautifully ornate, the kind that would make gentry salivate.
All clamored for her attention, but to none did she give her affection.
None, but one…none, but me… Robert James McGee.

Being the master of the *Scorpion*, known as the seas greatest champion,
Upon the Spanish Main, did indeed go against her father's grain!
He is a man of cardinal direction, who believes in "sublime perfection."

Thirty-two points he did give, on how "A God fearing man, should live!"
However, in me he saw no such qualities, and despite her pleas…
I was no longer welcome at his door, and was forbidden to see her…forevermore!

So with broken heart in tow, I returned to the sea's ebb and flow.
They say such things in time do fade, those fools know not of what love is made.
For death plucked my beloved Rose, even in this… my love for her, still grows.

Then one moonlit night, my eyes beheld a most radiant sight!
Standing on deck almost froze, was the translucent form of my Rose.
Therewith in dulcet tone, she sang a song we'd both had known.

Of our love…a love so rare…that nothing on earth can compare!
"Let this symbol be a sign, betwixt your heart and mine.
Every chart you course, and map you see, know that you are not that far from me!"

Shana L. Martin
©2008
Inspired By God & Syren AKA Kim

16

The Ghost and Captain Emerald
By Pamala A. Williams
©2009

Emerald smiled as she watched the delivery of the trunk. It was a beautiful old piece. And what a bargain. She loved dickering for a better price than the one asked. She directed the workmen as to where the trunk was to be set. It was heavy. She knew she couldn't lift it. It took two large men to carry it and they were huffing and puffing with the strain. She tossed them each a sovereign and dismissed them. Looking around, she saw that her crew was nowhere to be seen. That was good. They were all on shore leave, and wouldn't be back for a few more hours. That should give Emerald enough time to try to figure out how to get into the locked trunk with no keys.

The trunk was old. The wood was definitely oak. That was one reason it was so heavy. If she could get it open, she could see the contents. She was like a child at Yuletide. She just needed to get it open without damaging it. Emerald ran her fingers over the carvings. So beautiful. So artistic. There were sea creatures carved into the wood. Some, she recognized, some she didn't. Ships on ocean waves, wind billowing the sails. It smelled of the sea. The second hand shop she got it from was one she liked to frequent. There always seemed to be pieces there that were just for her.

The lock was an old one, but not too old. It had a bit of rust on it, but not bad. Maybe one of Diamond's keys would open it. Emerald left her cabin and went in search of Diamond's keys. She found some of the keys on Diamond's trunk near her hammock. Emerald took the keys to see if one of them might work.

Back in her cabin, with the door locked, Emerald worked all the keys. None seemed to work. She was about to give up when the very last key made a clicking sound inside the lock. The lock did not pop open, but Emerald wiggled and jiggled the key, and cursed her luck and finally the lock popped open.

18

Diamond had a lot of keys, and Emerald knew that not all of them were used aboard ship. She hoped this key was not one Diamond needed, and slipped it off the ring. She quickly took the rest of the keys back to where she found them, lest Diamond return and find them missing. Surely she wouldn't miss this one little key.

When she had returned to her cabin and locked herself in, she sat on the floor in front of the trunk and took a deep breath. Now she would find what she had paid five pounds for. She knew it was a steal, but that old reprobate of a shop keeper had wanted twice that much. He probably knew that someone would haggle the price down. Even if there was no key for the lock, the trunk was a piece of beauty. Well made and artistically carved, it would probably bring quite a bit in London. With a key, it would bring even more.

Emerald, however, did not plan on selling this trunk. It called to her. The moment she saw it, she knew she had to have it. There was something about it that set her imagination soaring. Someone's old sea trunk. What sights the owner must have seen. Taking another deep breath, Emerald gripped the trunk lid and hefted it open, propping the lid against the wall.

Sandalwood. The scent wrapped around her. She breathed it in. Looking in, she saw some old clothes. Taking them out one by one, she made a mental inventory. The old coat looked interesting. It was good wool, with one button missing. It was long enough to cover her knees, but would not impede her walking. This could come in handy when they were in the North Sea. A couple of shirts that looked like they might fit. A pair of breeches that in no way would fit her womanly hips. A couple of pair of stockings that had seen better days. Maybe Ruby could use them for something. A small wooden box.

Emerald took out the small wooden box and opened it. Her eyes grew wide as she gazed at the contents. There were several men's rings, with a number of different gems placed in them. These, she was sure, were worth much more than the five pounds she paid for them. She found several gold pieces, and there, on the bottom was a beautiful, tiny ring, looped on a velvet ribbon with a larger ring, and an even larger ring. How interesting. Emerald took the rings out. The middle sized ring fit her left ring finger perfectly. The smaller one just barely fit over the end of her pinky. The larger one was even bigger than her thumb. They were all three crafted alike, as if they were for a family, father, mother and child. Perhaps they belonged to the sailor whose trunk this had been. Emerald wondered about the previous owner of the trunk. What had happened to him? What of his family? Were they still alive?

Emerald placed the rings back inside the wooden box and put the box back inside the trunk. As she did, she noticed a tear in the bottom fabric. She tried to smooth the tear down, and realized that there was something sticking up out of the tear. Taking out her knife, she tried to get the object out of the fabric tear, and discovered a false bottom.

Taking out the contents of the trunk, she worked at pulling up the false bottom. There, in the bottom of this old trunk, was a small oval. It was painted with the likeness of a man, a woman and a child. The woman looked quite like Emerald, herself, but the eyes that looked back at her were blue, not green like Emerald's eyes. Her hair was a soft yellow, instead of the bright Irish red of her own. But the rest of the woman looked remarkably like Emerald. The child, a boy, she decided, was blond and small. An adorable smile. But it was the man that had her glued to the oval. A man with dark curly hair. Eyes, the color of a stormy sky. His complexion was dark as if he spent hours in the sun. The man's painted eyes seemed to bore into Emerald's. Her heart skipped a beat. No man had ever looked at her like that.

Emerald dropped the oval back into the trunk, and putting back the items she had taken out, she shut the lid. Well, at least she had discovered who the rings belonged to.

*　　　　*　　　　*　　　　*　　　　*

When the crew had returned from shore leave, Emerald went ashore in search of the local tavern. It was something she always did. She let the crew have some fun, then she went ashore for some as well. When she walked into the *Kettle's Spout* she was met by a group of men she knew.

"Well, would ya look at what the wind blew in, 'tis Cap'n Emerald herself," said a short man with grey hair and a pipe sticking out of his mouth.

"How're ye doing, Jocko? Missed ya last time I was here."

"Aye, well, we was up in Denmark. Haulin' some such for somebody. Cold as a whore's arse it was, too." Jocko let out a belly laugh that had all the tavern patrons joining in.

20

"Aye, that it is, Jocko, that it is. I'm feeling generous tonight Mike," she said to the barkeep, "whiskey all around." And she set a gold coin on the bar.

Mike picked up the coin, looked at it, bit it, and smiled. He started pouring glasses of whiskey for the patrons, and Katie, the barmaid, started handing them out.

"Where's the music? Can't have a good time without music," Emerald said.

From somewhere, a fiddle started to play a lively tune, followed by a concertina and a tin whistle. Soon the patrons were clapping in time with the music and a couple of them got up to do a jig. Someone threw a bodhrin to Emerald and she started keeping a good beat going. Someone stuck a cigar in Emerald's mouth and lit it and the whiskey flowed.

A little before dawn, Emerald had made her way back to the ship and collapsed into her bunk. She hadn't been asleep very long when she heard a soft voice call, "Emmerine."

She sat up. "Whaa? No, Emerald. Not Emmerine. Who said that?"

"Emmerine," the voice said again.

Emerald looked all around. She was alone in her cabin.

"Emmerine," the voice called.

"Who's there? Show yerself." Emerald slid off her bunk and grabbed her cutlass. She searched her entire cabin, but there was no one there. She opened her cabin door and looked out. She could see no one lurking outside her cabin. Shrugging, Emerald closed the door, put away her cutlass, and lay back down n the bed.

"Emmerine," the voice called softly.

"All right, ye blighter. Stand and be recognized. I need sleep, and I'll not stand for this nonsense. Show yerself."

All was quiet in Emerald's cabin except for her heavy breathing. She was not happy at being awakened by someone she couldn't find. There was a knock on the door.

"Blast," Emerald said as she made her way to the door. "What the devil do ye…oh, Topaz, what do ye need?"

"Well, Cap'n, ye told us we were shipping off today, but ye didn't tell us where we're going. Coral needs a heading. We've pulled away from the dock, but we need to know where we're going."

Emerald sighed. "Sorry. Had other things on me mind. Head for Rotterdam. We're to pick up a shipment of cheese. I need sleep."

"Aye, Cap'n. I'll not be bothering ye again until we reach Rotterdam."

Topaz sauntered off, and Emerald closed the door to her cabin. She climbed back into her bunk and fell asleep.

The ship shuddered and lurched, nearly throwing Emerald out of her bunk. She got up and made her way to the door, weaving as she went to stay afoot. When she opened the door a wave came over the gunwale and washed across the deck.

"Blast and double blast." She grabbed her slicker and hurried up to the capstan. Coral was having a hell of a time trying to keep the wheel from spinning amok. "Why didn't someone come get me?" she asked.

Coral tugged with all her might. "Just came up all the sudden like. Haven't had time yet."

Emerald took the wheel from Coral and steered her vessel through the storm.

*   *   *   *   *

When the storm had passed, the Salty Kiss was beached on an unknown island somewhere south of England. Emerald did not recognize it. She had no way of knowing just how far the storm had blown them. Emerald was exhausted. She untied the lashing from around her waist. Separated herself from the mizzen mast. Her ship was a mess. The top of the main mast was broken off, the sails in tatters.

"Diamond! Ruby! Anyone?"

The hatch opened, and Topaz stepped out onto the deck. She looked around. "Oh, Captain. Look at the ship. Oh, my Lord. Are ye alright, Captain?"

"Aye, Topaz. I just be so tired. Is everyone else all right?"

"Not sure, yet. I just came to, meself."

Ruby came on deck. "Oh, Cap'n. Look at the sails. We'll never be able to go anywhere with sails like this."

Ruby sported a small cut on her cheek. "Ye be fine, then Ruby?"

Ruby looked back at the captain. "Aye. A might sore, but I'll live to see another day. And you, Cap'n? Be ye well?"

"Better than the ship. Spread out, we must find the rest of the crew." Topaz and Ruby started looking for the rest of the crew members as Emerald looked to her ship. Would she ever get her ship repaired? It looked to be too much for a crew of women. But this was her home. She would see it once more on the seas, or she would die trying.

"Cap'n," cried Ruby.

Emerald looked to Ruby, she was at the rail looking on the shore and pointing. Emerald made her way to Ruby. There, lying on the sand with the water softly caressing their feet were several crew members. There were also casks, splintered wood and other debris from the ship, from the storm.

"Hurry, let's get down and see if the live." Emerald and Ruby climbed down a hastily thrown rope ladder to the shore. Pearl was sitting up when they got to her. She was looking around disoriented.

"Cap'n? That was some storm." She broke off to cough up some of the sea water she had apparently swallowed. "I would just a soon not go in another one like that, if ye do not mind."

Emerald smiled. "I agree with ye, Pearl. Let's not go into another storm like that. We need to find the others."

Pearl stood, wobbly at first. Ruby was checking on the next person she found on the sand. Pearl went to help her.

"Captain, we need you up here, hurry." Emerald looked up and saw Topaz at the railing motioning for her to come.

Emerald looked back at the shore, Ruby was helping Coral sit up, Pearl was checking on Opal. She could see Sapphire lying on the sand. There were no others that she could see. "Check the other side of the ship when yer done here," she commanded. Pearl and Ruby nodded. Emerald turned and climbed back up onto the deck.

Topaz took Emerald's arm.

"Garnet's pinned by one of the guns."

Emerald ran to the hold and hurried down to the gun ports. Several of the guns had broken loose and were scattered about. One poked through a hole in the side that hadn't been there before the storm. Bloodstone stood, holding an obviously broken arm, while she tried to tie a rope onto the gun so they could pull it off of Garnet. Jade, with blood all over one arm, was helping. Emerald hurried over to Garnet.

"Garnet, can ye hear me?" she asked.

"Aye, Cap'n. Can ye get the bleeding thing off. It hurts something powerful."

Emerald checked to see if she could see the damage. Luckily, she saw no blood. With luck, Garnet had not suffered permanent damage. She took the rope from Jade and Bloodstone. She heaved with all her might, and the gun moved enough for Bloodstone to drag Garnet from her prison.

"Thank ye, kindly, Cap'n." And Garnet promptly fainted.

"We need to get her out of here before any more of these things decide to break loose." She looked at Jade and Bloodstone. "Have you seen Diamond or Amethyst? " They both shook their heads.

"Topaz, get these three up on deck. Be careful with Garnet."

"Aye, Captain. Jade, get her feet. Bloodstone, try to keep her middle up. I'll get her head and shoulders."

Emerald went down into the hold. She saw Onyx sitting on an overturned barrel. "Onyx?"

"Me shoulder, Captain. I think it's either broken or out of socket. It's hurting right good."

Emerald nodded. "Go up on deck. Have Topaz check it out for you."

Onyx assented and started up to the deck. Emerald looked about for Amethyst and Diamond. She headed for the brig. Knowing Diamond, she would check to make sure any prisoners were safe, and the only one in there was Amethyst. She had returned to the ship in a disreputable shape. She was only supposed to sleep it off.

Emerald saw Amethyst come up for air. The brig area was under water. With tears in her eyes, Amethyst said, "I can't find her. She has to be there, but I can't find her."

"If she's been in there since the storm, Amethyst, she's lost to us.

"No, Captain, she slipped in only moments ago. And I can't find her."

Emerald dove into the water. The water was cold and black. Emerald could see nothing. But her friend was in danger, and she wouldn't stop until she found her. Out of air, Emerald surfaced, gulped in air, and dove in again. She had to find Diamond. Her outthrust hand touched something soft and she grabbed and pulled it to her. She felt Diamond's arm and she pulled with all her might, but it wouldn't budge. Not letting go, she surfaced again. "Amethyst, I've found her, but she's caught on something. Come hold her, so we don't lose her. I will try to get her lose."

Amethyst swam toward the captain, and grabbed hold of Diamond's arm, then Emerald dove down to free Diamond. She found it. The lacings from the bow on Diamond's bodice were caught on the hinge of the brig. Taking the knife out of its sheath, she cut the bow and tugged on Diamond's clothes to bring her to the surface. Amethyst and Emerald pulled her out of the water and onto the dry, tilted floor.

"She not be breathing," cried Amethyst.

Emerald laid her hand on Diamond's neck. She could detect a faint pulse. She had not been captain of her own ship and not learned a thing or three about doctoring. Oftentimes she and the cook were the only ones who did know. She cut the laces of Diamond's bodice loose, and before she could do more, Diamond spit up a mouthful of water, and gulped in air. Diamond's eyes rolled back in her head and she flopped back down on the floor.

Amethyst began to wail. "She's dead, and it's all my fault. She would not even be down here if it were not for me."

Emerald rolled her eyes. "Amethyst, Diamond is not dead."

"Aye, she is," she sobbed. "I could not find her. I tried, but I could not find her. And now she's gone."

"Did ye no see her take a breath? She lives."

"No, she is dead and it is all my fault. I should not have come back to the ship drunk. I knew she would throw me in gaol, but I drank anyway. Oh, now what are we to do? Diamond is dead."

Emerald had had all she could take of Amethyst's nonsense. "Amethyst. Be ye injured?"

Amethyst shook her head. "No, Captain, a might shaken up, but unharmed, thanks to Diamond." And she started wailing again.

Emerald slapped Amethyst across the face. "Ye bleeding ninny. She lives, I tell ye. Look at her chest. See the rise and fall of her breaths? She could not be doing that if she were dead. Now help me get her up on deck, with the rest of the injured."

Amethyst held her palm against her injured cheek. Her eyes were wide and her mouth hung open. After hearing Emerald tell her yet again that Diamond was indeed alive, she quickly helped her captain take her injured crewmate topside.

*   *   *   *   *

Emerald was exhausted. A ship wreck was one thing. She counted herself lucky that the only members of the crew that were missing were the two bilge rats that she had shang…uh, picked up in the last port they had been in. She wasn't sure if the storm got them, or they jumped ship when they beached. At any rate, they were unimportant. Her crew, although some with injuries, was alive and all accounted for.

After tending to the injured, a make-shift shelter was erected on deck using the tattered sails. Onyx and Bloodstone were able to find enough usable ship's stores to feed everyone. After posting a watch and setting a watch schedule, Emerald made her way to her disheveled cabin and collapsed in her bunk. She had been asleep no more than a few minutes when a soft voice called.

"Emmerine."

Emerald awoke and winced. Not again.

"Emmerine."

"Go away. I need me sleep."

"Emmerine."

"Go away, I tell ye. It's been one hell of a day, and I dinna need more of yer blather. Pipe down and let me sleep."

The voice quieted. Sometime after the second watch had started, Emerald felt someone touch her shoulder.

"Hmmm? Is it time for me watch?" She sat up and looked around. The cabin was dark, but enough moonlight filtered in that she saw she was alone. She looked around. Someone had just touched her shoulder. Her cabin door was closed and she knew that whoever had awaken her had not had time to leave.

"What's going on here? Am I losing me bleeding mind?"

"Emmerine." The voice called softly.

Emerald was out of her bunk in a flash. "All right. I have had it. Show yerself. I am tired of this blessed game ye be playing."

From the trunk, a bluish white glow emerged. The trunk had not closed all the way. Something blocked the lid from closing. The glow grew until it was as tall, then taller than Emerald. She stood her ground, but she was clearly frightened. The glow began to take shape, and soon, a transparent man stood before her.

"Emmerine," he said. He held out a hand to her.

Emerald tried to take a step back, but she was up against her bunk. "The name is Emerald, not Emmerine. Who are ye, and who is Emmerine.?"

"You are not Emmerine? But where is she? I must find Emmerine." The spirit appeared to study Emerald. "You look like Emmerine. Why do you insist you are not her? You must be Emmerine. Have you injured yourself, my darling, and forgotten your name?"

"I nae be anyone's darling. I have not injured meself, and my name is Emerald. Who do you be?"

The spirit, ghost, or whatever you want to call it appeared to be distressed. "How can that be? It was Emmerine who was to find me. The storm was to take us home."

"Storm? You conjured up that bleeding storm? The storm that wrecked my ship and nearly cost me my crew?" Emerald's eyes flashed with pent up anger. "Why ye blasted figment, I'll roast ye in hot oil, I'll set yer hair on fire, I'll…I'll…"

"Please, dear lady. My apologies. I did not mean to cause you stress."

"Stress, ye say? Stress? I will be causing ye some stress." Emerald stopped and looked at the ghost. He looked a might familiar. Her eyes widened. The trunk.

"Be ye the one who owned the sea trunk?"

The ghost looked at Emerald, and then behind him at the trunk. Smiling, he said, "Yes, that is my trunk. It is opened. You have looked inside?"

"Of course. I paid good money for that trunk. Ye think I was just going to use it as a paper weight?"

"And the…the portrait. You saw that as well?"

Emerald nodded. "That be you and yer family?

"My wife, Emmerine, and our son, Mikal. My name is Donali. I have been trying to get home. The ship I was on was lost at sea."

"But yer a spook. Surely yer home be Heaven, now."

"Heaven? Hmm. No, I do not believe so. I must return home to Saladan. That is my home."

Emerald closed her eyes. "Jesus, Mary and Joseph, now I be talking to spooks. Sure and I've lost me mind."

Donali looked at Emerald concerned, and then he smiled. "Ah, I think I understand, now. Are you not from the land called Ireland?"

"Aye, that I am. And I will tell ye now, I have heard of no port called Saladan."

"That explains much. You say you paid good money for my trunk. Is that right?"

"Aye, five pounds it was. 'Tis a beautiful trunk, to be sure."

"And where, dear lady, did you buy my trunk?"

"In Talbot's used goods shop in Portsmouth, England."

The ghost shook his head. "Something went wrong. It was not supposed to go anywhere but home. How did it end up there, do you suppose?"

"That I canna say, but when I saw the trunk, I had to buy it. 'Tis one of the most beautiful things I have ever seen."

"Dear lady, Emerald, if I may. If my calculations have been correct, your ship should have landed near my home. Shall we go out on deck? I would like to have a look around."

"I suppose we could do that. Although I urge you to be quiet. Several of my crew members have been injured in the storm, and I will not have you cause them any added stress."

"To be sure. I will keep to your shoulder and speak to no one but you." With that said, the spirit laid his hand on her shoulder and shrank to the size of a mouse. He stood on Emerald's shoulder and held on to her hair.

"I just a soon ye not be doing that. It is a bit creepy, if ye know what I mean."

"I understand, but so as not to distress your crew, it is best that no one else sees me. Please, Dear Emerald, lead on."

Emerald left her cabin and went out on the deck. It was dark, and Onyx was checking on a few of the crew. "How are they?" asked Emerald.

"Bloodstone's arm is broken, Sapphire has a broken leg. I've sewn up the gash in Jade's arm. Garnet has few broken ribs, and she will be sore for a while. Diamond still has not awakened, yet. My shoulder was just dislocated, and Topaz was able to get it back in place, but it hurts like hell. The rest are mostly cuts and bruises. I'm concerned about Garnet, but I think she will be fine. I am worried about Diamond, though. We will just have to wait and see."

Emerald nodded. She walked to the rail and looked out at the island.

"This is Saladan," Donali said softly. "I'm sure of it."

"If this be yer home," said Emerald just as softly, "why has no one come? Especially if they were expecting ye to arrive by storm."

"They will come in the morning."

"Have ye healers, there? For me crew."

"We have the finest healers in all the world. Excellent carpenters, as well. I will make sure that your ship is repaired, although it will probably take a little time."

"I thank ye. The ship is my home, but the crew....they be my friends, ye kin?"

"I understand. When my people come, they will have to take my truck to the beach. It has to touch our soil for me to come back."

"Come back?"

"Yes. To live again."

Emerald stared at the beach. "I dinnae kin what ye mean. Ye are dead. How can ye live again?"

"Oh, but I am not dead. I am only in an altered state. When the ship I was on was in distress, I sent a message home to Emmerine. Then, I changed. I knew my love would find me. But alas, I was mistaken. It was you, and not my Emmerine. For that, I shall be forever in your debt."

"I dinnae kin what ye mean by an altered state."

"It is most difficult to explain. My race is far advanced to your own. We can will our bodies to do far more than you can. I, in essence, turned myself into a wisp, an essence of my being. This, I placed inside my trunk. Myself and Emmerine have the only keys. When my trunk was opened, my essence was then allowed to escape. Had I been on my home soil, I would have then turned myself back into my corporeal self. However, that transformation cannot happen until I am on my home soil. I hope that explanation helps."

"Not really, but I will take your word for it." Emerald gazed out at the island. There was a pleasant breeze blowing from the sea, and the trees swayed slightly. It was quite a bit warmer than England, and she still wondered how far the storm had blown them. "I need to get some sleep. Would ye be a nice wisp and retire to yer trunk whilst I sleep?"

"Of course, dear Emerald. We can do nothing until morning."

Emerald walked back to her cabin, noting her sleeping crew as she went. Once in her cabin, Donali retreated to his trunk. Emerald shut the lid. She did not want any intrusions from him as she slept. She took off her bodice and boots and collapsed onto her tilted bunk. She was asleep almost instantaneously.

* * * * *

The next morning, she awoke with a start. Someone had knocked on her cabin door. Wearily, she climbed out of her bunk and went to the door. She opened it to find Amethyst excited hopping from foot to foot.

"I have no head in me cabin, Amethyst. If the head be underwater, ye best climb down to the beach and find yer own privy."

Amethyst gaped at Emerald, then turned red. "Nae, Captain. I do not need to use the privy, well yes I do, but that is not why I am so excited. There are people coming up the beach. People! Coming here!" And she ran to the railing and pointed up the beach.

Emerald followed and stood at the railing and watched the people head for the ship. There were perhaps ten people in all. Among them, she saw a woman with long blond hair wearing a green gown. *That must be Emmerine,* she thought. The crew was stirring, except for Garnet and Diamond. Garnet was awake, but in too much pain to move about. Diamond had still not awaken.

"Ahoy, the ship," called a man with a strange accent.

Emerald waved. "Welcome. We have injured. I hope you brought a healer."

"Permission to board?"

"Aye."

Several men climbed up the rope ladder that was still hanging off the side of the ship. When the man who had hailed alighted on the deck, he walked up to Emerald and bowed. "My name is Morganet. Welcome to Saladan. I believe you have brought a trunk to us?"

"Aye, I have yer trunk. The storm that Donali conjured up was a bad one. I dinnae know how far off course it blew us, but you can see some of the damage to me ship. And several of me crew is injured. He promised it would all be set to rights."

"And it shall. You have spoken to Donali? How is that possible? Emmerine has the only other key to the trunk."

"Well, I bought the trunk, and worried the lock until it opened. Yer spook mistook me for his Emmerine."

"There is a remarkable resemblance. And where may the trunk be?"

"Tis in me cabin, but ye will not be taking it until a healer sees to me crew." Emerald crossed her arms over her chest and stood with her legs apart. No one was going to do anything aboard her ship without her permission. The ship may be wrecked, but it was still her ship. She was still the captain of it.

Morganet said something to one of the men in a language that Emerald had never heard before. The man bowed to Emerald and went to the first crew member. He took a strange looking instrument from a bag he had slung over his shoulder. He waved it over Sapphire's leg, then took out something else from his bag and touched her leg in several places. He smiled at

Sapphire, patted her shoulder and moved on to Jade. He repeated the process with the injured crew until he came to Garnet.

As he passed the first instrument over Garnet's middle, he turned to Morganet and frowned. He said something to him. Morganet turned to Emerald. "Antelli tells me that that woman has a serious injury. She is bleeding inside."

Emerald gasped and turned to look at Garnet. Garnet was very pale. She turned back to Morganet. "Can ye help her?"

"Yes, but we will need to take her to our city. There we have better equipment than Antelli could bring. We must do so right away. She could perish, if we do not." Morganet turned toward Antelli as he said something else. He had moved to Diamond. "Antelli tells me that the other woman should go with us to the city as well. She is not as serious as the other, but needs more attention that we can give her here. The rest of your crew will be fine. Antelli has mended the broken bones and tissue. You will all be our guests while we repair your ship. It is the least we can do for bringing Donelli back to us."

Morganet went to the railing and called down in his strange language and the people still on the beach began moving around and doing things that Emerald had no knowledge of. When he turned back to Emerald, he said, "My people will take the injured ones to the city. Where is the trunk?"

Emerald led him to her cabin. He went straight to the trunk. The lock hung open, but the lid was closed. He opened the lid, and Donali wisped out.

"Donali, it is good to have you back. We will get you to the beach in mere moments. Emmerine awaits you there."

"Morganet, it is truly good to see you, my friend. I have many stories to tell. Pray, did you help these fine people?"

"Antelli has healed all but two. Alas, they must be healed in the city. We have sent for litters. The men await to bring your trunk to the beach."

"Very well." With that, Donali wisped back into the trunk. Morganet called to two men who came into Emerald's cabin, hefted the trunk and carried it out on deck. Emerald put her boots and bodice on and followed them out, lacing herself into her bodice as she went.

The men had set up a block and tackle and wrapped the trunk with rope and lowered it to the beach. Emmerine ran to the trunk, noting that the lock was open, and opened the lid. Emerald watched as Donali wisped out of the trunk and alighted on the beach. In the blink of an eye, he changed back into a man. Emerald gaped in astonishment. Never had she seen nor even dreamed anything as fantastic as what she had just witnessed. Then, she heard some buzzing. The buzzing sound grew louder and louder until she could see what was causing the sound. There were two contraptions flying up the beach toward the ship. They were both in the shape of hammerhead sharks, but there were men inside them. Emerald's heart beat fast as she wasn't certain whether to fight the things or just watch.

Morganet saw her face and placed a hand on her arm. "Do not fear. These are the litters that will take your injured to the city. I will take you there. Let us all go down to the beach. I am sure that Emmerine will wish to thank you for bringing Doneli home."

"I will not be going anywhere until I know that Garnet and Diamond are safely on their way to your city."

Emerald watched as the litters alighted on the deck and the men gently placed the two crew members in the litters. Then the litters began to buzz again and took off from the deck and flew back down the beach.

"I cannae believe what I be seeing. Flying sharks. 'Tis truly a dream I be havin'."

Morganet smiled. "Come, Captain. We will show you more things for you to dream about."

Everyone descended the rope ladder and when Emerald touched to the beach, Donalli and Emmerine strode up to her. Donali clasped both of her hands in his. "Thank you, dear Emerald, for finding me and bringing me home."

"I may have found ye, but ye be the one who brought us here. Although I dinnae kin where here is."

Emmerine came forward and peered at Emerald. She said something to Donali in their strange language. Donali smiled and nodded. "My Emmerine is very surprised at how much the two of you look alike. We would like you to be our guests while your ship is being repaired.

The two women who were taken to our hospital should be well in a day or two, and they will come to our home as well."

"I thank ye. When will repairs start on me ship?"

"Preparations are under way as we speak. There should be a crew here in a matter of moments to begin repairs."

*   *   *   *   *

Emerald stood on a terrace and gazed out at the magnificent city below. It was silver and gold, shining in the sun. Several flying "sharks" were about ferrying people and things to places she could not even imagine. There were trees and exotic plants everywhere. Colorful birds flew in the skies.

Donali and Emmerine came to stand beside her. Emerald looked at them with the wide eyes of a child on Yuletide.

"What wonders there be. What is this place?"

"This is the city of Saladan, on the island of Atlantis. This has been home to my people for eons."

"Eons?"

"More years than you can imagine." Donali smiled.

"I have heard of this Atlantis. 'Tis said to have sunk into the ocean thousands of years ago."

"Sunk?" Donali seemed to ponder the possibility. "I suppose you could say that. Actually, it was engineered to appear to sink. The Greeks and the Phoenicians were a lot of bother. It was the only way we could think of to get them to leave us alone. We are an island that moves."

"How can an island move?" asked Emerald.

"Ah, dear Captain. I cannot be giving away our secrets. But suffice it to say, we are where we want to be, when we want to be there. Our civilization has advanced far beyond your own. Sometimes, I am not so sure it is all for the good. We have had our problems, as with all civilizations. But one thing we have learned is to keep an open mind. There are many mysteries on this planet, and one can never learn the answer to them all. Even we, who have been searching for answers for eons, have not learned all we want to know. Love is one of the most moving forces of all time. Love was what brought me back to my home. With your help, of course."

Emerald smiled. This was truly a remarkable place.

"If you listen with your heart, you will hear the songs of the trees, the flowers, the mountains. There is magic all around us. I have found that most people in your civilization believe that magic is not real any more. They are blind to it. They have turned their backs on it. It is there. It exists. It will not go away, no matter if people believe or not. It is. Believe, Emerald. Listen with your heart. You will see the magic. You will hear the things most people do not hear. You will feel. You will know."

Emerald shivered. Magic? Real? She could only gape at Donali and Emmerine.

"Can you show me?"

Donali smiled sadly and shook his head. "No. I am sorry, but it is not my place to show you. It is only in you. You must seek. You must search for it. It is there. It waits for you to find it."

"But how will I know?"

Donali looked into Emmerine's eyes and smiled. He raised her hands and kissed her fingertips. Looking at Emerald he said, "When you find it, you will know. It waits for you, Emerald. Magic is very personal. Once you find it, your heart will sing with gladness. But you must be careful not to abuse it. Abuse magic, and it will turn on you. Magic is a wonderful thing. It can also be terrifying. Some of us have discovered that the hard way."

"Mayhap I will leave the magic to the magicians. If it can conjure up a storm like the one that sent us here, I dinnae think I want to be fiddling with it."

*   *   *   *   *

Two days later, Diamond and Garnett were out of the hospital and recovering. Emerald was very relieved that her friends and crewmates were going to be all right.

"Emerald," Donali said as she stood on the balcony talking to the crew.

"Oh aye, Donali, I thank ye for having me crew taken care of. I dinnae know what I would have done had I lost one of them."

Donali smiled and bowed. "You are most welcome. I have news of your ship."

Emerald was at his side in an instant. "Me ship? Is there a problem with the repairs? Can ye not fix it?"

Donali laughed. "On the contrary, Dear Emerald. Your ship repairs are completed. It stands at the ready. At this moment, supplies are being loaded for your journey back to England."

"So fast? You truly are amazing. I thought it would take months for the repairs to me ship."

"We are nothing, if not efficient. "

Emerald bowed and gathered up her crew. Donali had several flying sharks take the crew back to the beach where the Salty Kiss was anchored. Supply sharks were coming and going off the deck. Finally, only one shark remained, and that was Donali's.

"Emerald. There will be no memory of me or Saladan. We cannot risk discovery by your world. But I want you to know that you have my eternal thanks for bringing me home."

"'Twas you that conjured up that devil storm. But you are most welcome. I am glad that you found your Emmerine. But sad I will be with no memory of this place. This Atlantis is a sight to be sure. 'Tis most beautiful. Mayhap we will see one another in future?"

Donali clasped Emerald's hand, raised it to his lips and brushed a soft kiss across her knuckles. He smiled as he said, "Mayhap."

Donali climbed back aboard his flying shark and left the deck of the Salty Kiss. Before his shark had touched the beach, a fog blew up, shrouding the Kiss. Emerald could see nothing that was not in front of her. When the fog cleared, there was no island in sight. The Salty Kiss tossed about in the sea as Emerald found her hands on the ship's wheel. She pulled out her compass and looked at it. Seeing that she was headed in a north-northeast direction, she continued on her way.

"Captain, it appears that storm blew us off course a little. That appears to be the coast of northern France. We'll be a day or two late arriving in Rotterdam." Coral was standing ready to take the helm.

"Aye," Emerald said. "A day or two late." Apparently Coral didn't remember being on the island, but Emerald did. Resolved to keep the secret of Atlantis, Emerald turned to Coral, relinquishing the helm. "Aye, well the cheese will still be there. It will no go bad in this short of time.

"Topaz," she called out to her first mate. "Make haste. We've cheese to pick up in Holland. I feel the need of some ale from a pub. The Arm and Hammer in Rotterdam seems to be calling me name."

Topaz began shouting orders to the crew. Emerald smiled as she made her way back to her cabin. Atlantis. Imagine that. It does exit. Aye, she would keep Donali's secret. To her grave.

Nameless Enemy

I stand over your lifeless body,
A red-dripping sword in my hand,
The battle around me is ending:
Your captain has yielded his command.

I consider your face and your costume;
You come from another world indeed.
You are completely foreign to me,
Except that we both can bleed.

I begin to join my shipmates –
But your face catches my eye.
A strange feeling starts to come o'er me,
It's hard to explain but I'll give it a try.

I know that in life we were enemies,
Your ship and mine in battle met.
My blood was in jeopardy as I faced you;
I should revile you and hate you and yet . . .

As I stand here I recall our meeting;
You rushed to the fight without fear.
You fought with courage and ably
Protecting this ship you held dear.

You wear a necklace of gold with a ruby
And wield a sword that was excellently made;
And I can tell by the way that you used it,
You were a man who made a living with the blade

You fought me with all that was in you,
And you fought with a smile on your face.
Your sword arm never truly failed you
But it was I that was the victor in our race.

You died without a cry or a whimper,
You fought till you died where you stood,
Answering the call of your captain,
As a man of honor always should.

I cannot abide your religion
And your country is at war with mine,
But you didn't choose your heritage
And to our fates we must all resign.

Another life might have made us different:
Shipmates, chums, or dear friends.
But my God in His infinite wisdom
Saw fit to bring our lives to these ends –

You lying there dead in red ruin;
Me standing with your blood on my boot,
But to you, a brave nameless enemy,
I raise my sword in silent salute.

Life is full of questions without answers,
Some mysteries we can never dispel,
But I am sure we both honored the proverb:
"Live each day and, by God, live it well!"

Stephen Sanders
©2009

Cursed Few

Many have shared a tale,
Of men and women who climb rigging and hoist sail.
Some have triumphed over squall and gail,
Most try and most fail.

Still if you think you are up to snuff,
Dare ye call a man's bluff
And say he, "Doesn't have the stuff!"
He'll cut out your tongue to say, "That's enough!"

A mother's warning be unto you,
For those who wish to sail the ocean blue.
Beware of the pirate crew, known as…
The Cursed Few!

Shana L. Martin
©2008
Inspired by God & The Crew Known as "Cursed Few"

The Frigate Grey Ghost

Where'er the wind roars ---
Cross Maldives to Seychelles,
Round Cape Horn to the blustery Azores,
From the Antipodes to the frigid Poles
Cross twenty-four time zones,
This is the ship, the Frigate *Grey Ghost*,
Which scatters men's bones.
With mugs of Madeira or Portuguese Rum
Or mugs of warm rain in the scuttlebutt room ---
From Maine to the Barbary Coast,
Let all Pirates now join in a toast:

"There be Ships most elusive,
        But none of them close
For the Frigate we sail
        Be the Mighty *Grey Ghost*!"

From out of the mists, from out of the fog,
From out of God knows where
Comes the Frigate *Grey Ghost*
And its Captain Robespierre.
At the helm of the Ghost
Steers her Captain who boasts:

"With me Letters of Marque
        We sail over the shallows and over the depths
And escape from the gallows
        If ever we're caught!"

"So, raise the top-gallants, Me Hearties!
The mains and the royals!
Lay into the wind till the seawater boils,
Plot me a path straightway to the coast.
There's a ship to be boarded for profit and fun,
And no one outruns the Frigate *Grey Ghost*!"

"There be Ships most elusive,
       But none of them close
For the Frigate we sail
       Be the Mighty *Grey Ghost*!"

"Raise the black flag of Camellia and Rose –
The Red of the Blood and the Black of the Night! –
That tops our ship's mast wherever she goes!
So pull out the wedges and run out the guns!
We do battle with many and win over most,
For no ship can escape the Frigate *Grey Ghost*!"

"There be Ships most elusive,
       But none of them close
For the Frigate we sail
       Be the Mighty *Grey Ghost*!"

Bobby Matherne
©2008

The Ocean Rolls On

The ocean rolls on . . .

I dream my greatest dream
I marry the love of my life
I plan my greatest triumph
I begin a great family

The ocean rolls on . . .

My dream turns into a nightmare
My love turns sour and dies
My triumph becomes a tragedy
My loss destroys my family entire

The ocean rolls on . . .

I lift myself up
I start over again
I bear life's darkest hours
I pray to God to save my soul

The ocean rolls on . . .

My reality becomes enough
My love finds a sweet, safe home
My struggle triumphs to victory
My legacy is born in a promise

The ocean rolls on and on . . .

Stephen Sanders
©2009

43

Maiden Of The Sea

James McShane had but one aim;
To find that which ignites desire's flame.
If only he knew her name…

Maiden, maiden, of the sea
Come to me, oh come to me.
My heart is full of love for thee.
Maiden, maiden, of the sea.

So he set sail on the seven,
 Upon the month, and well past the hour of eleven.
In search for "that gift from heaven!"

Maiden, maiden, of the sea
Come to me, oh come to me.
My heart is full of love for thee.
Maiden, maiden, of the sea.

With his spyglass he did gaze;
Through the mist and haze,
He saw her tail slowly raise.

Maiden, maiden, of the sea
Come to me, oh come to me.
My heart is full of love for thee.
Maiden, maiden, of the sea.

Then he glimpsed her face so fair;
While she combed her long auburn hair.
In voice strong he did declare…

Maiden, maiden, of the sea
Come to me, oh come to me.
My heart is full of love for thee.
Maiden, maiden, of the sea.

She swam on never to realize,
 As his salty tears stung his eyes.
Unable to hear his cries…

Maiden, maiden, of the sea
Come to me, oh come to me.
My heart is full of love for thee.
Maiden, maiden, of the sea.

Shana L. Martin
©2008
Inspired by God
Dedicated to "The Empty Hats"

JUDGMENT
By Pamala A. Williams
©2009

I stood with my hat in my hands before a tall desk. The man at the desk had white hair and an intelligent face. I felt his eyes bore into me. I felt exposed. This man held my fate in his hands.

"Do you know why you are here?" he asked.

I lowered my head, ashamed. "Aye, your Worship."

"I want you to explain your actions," he demanded, not unkindly.

"During the battle, Sir?" I asked.

"Yes. During the battle."

I nodded. "Well, Sir, we was making our way to port when the lookout spotted a ship on the horizon. The captain steered in the direction of the ship. When we got a bit closer, the lookout spotted her flag. It was French. Well, now, that got the captain intrigued, as it were. On account of the captain's sworn enemy is French.

"When we got closer still, the lookout could make out that it was the *Marie Cecile.* That's Captain Robere Le Clair's ship. He being Captain Snyder's enemy, ya see.

"So, Captain Snyder calls us all to battle stations. We're taking the *Marie Cecile,* he says. Ya see, Sir, Captain Snyder had a lovely wife. Pretty as a picture, she was. Only Captain Le Clair kind of took to her. 'Course she wouldn't have anything to do with him as she loved Captain Snyder. But Le Clair tried to force himself on her and Captain Snyder heard her screaming, he did, and started fighting Le Clair. Only Le Clair now, he didn't fight fair. Captain Snyder was using his fists and Le Clair pulls out a pistol and shoots Mrs. Snyder dead and stabs Captain Snyder in the chest. Captain Snyder lived, but vowed to see Le Clair dead.

46

"So when we know that the ship be Le Clair's, well Captain Snyder wants his revenge. Only Le Clair sees us coming and recognizes our ship as belonging to Snyder. We run up the colors and prepare for battle but Le Clair turns toward us and shoots his cannons at us. We got hit by a couple of balls and before we know it, Le Clair's men are boarding us."

"You killed a man. Do you feel no remorse?

"Well, now Sir, I don't take kindly with killing. I'm a gentle man, ye see. But that man I killed was trying to kill one of me shipmates. True, I don't much care for Humphries, but he's one of me shipmates and that there Frenchy was trying to kill him. I felt it was me duty to do what I could for him.

"But me main concern was for Nibs and Crawford. They are me friends, ye see. Shipmates, aye, but more. Friends. I knew they were in gaol. They had gotten drunk in port and Captain was making them stay in gaol until we got back to our home port. Docking their pay and all, as well. As I said, I knew they were in gaol, and I feared for them. What with a battle going on with them Frenchies and all. So I rush below to see to me friends. I know I should have stayed on deck and fought with the frogs, but me friends needed me.

"When I got to the gaol, they were fair to swimming, they were. The ship had taken on quite a bit of water. Now me? I never learned 'ow to swim. But me friends were in trouble. I took the keys off the hook and waded in. Nibs and Crawford were near to crying, they was afeared they'd drown. I unlocked the door and helped them out.

"We didn't make it back up before Le Clair let loose with another cannon volley. Fair to rocked the ship, it did. I remember I fell off the ladder leading up. Sorry, Sir, but I don't remember no more."

"You helped rescue your friends with no thought to your own safety?"

"Truth, yer Worship, Sir, I wasn't thinking about me. Only how they was trapped and someone had to get them out. They would have done the same for me."

"You are a pirate. That is against the law."

"Aye, Sir. A pirate. But I was a blacksmith afore that. It's just that the king took everything I had in taxes. It was either pirate or go to the poor house. You seen them poor houses, Sir? Pitiful they is. A death sentence for sure."

"And pirating isn't a death sentence?"

"For most, I suppose. But it's also hope, Sir. And freedom."

"You performed a noble deed is saving your friends' lives, but do you think it is enough to weigh against piracy?"

"Can't say, your Honor, Sir. That be something that's up to you, Sir."

"William Campbell, you are an honorable man."

"Thank ye, Sir, but, yer Honor, Sir?"

"Yes?"

"Me friends. Did they survive?"

"Yes, William. They live."

"Ah, good. Then it was worth it."

"You truly believe that, William?"

"Aye, Sir. I did what was right by them."

The man looked at me, then marked something in a book. He motioned to someone and he talked to him real low so I couldn't hear.

"William Campbell, please go with this gentleman and he will help get you settled in your new home, and give you your work assignments."

"Aye, Sir."

I followed the young man wondering what the judge had decided. I wondered what kind of work assignments I'd be given. The hallway led to two doors, side by side. One was painted black, and one was painted white. He opened the white door and held it open for me.

"Welcome to Heaven, William. I think you'll be happy here."

"Batson! BATSON! Get in here before I have your skin peeled from your back for shirking!"

The shout was coming from the office at the end of the hall and I knew that I'd better comply or Captain Griffin would, without a doubt, carry out his threat. I rose from the stool on which I had been sitting and, at a run, nearly flew down the hall to the open door. Arriving there, I was witness to a scene that was totally foreign to the Captain's office and his nature.

To begin with, the Captain was standing in front of his desk instead of sitting behind it. If this wasn't unusual enough, in his chair, was a woman. And she was crying.

Standing next to the crying woman was an older man, dressed in the clothes of a laborer, perhaps even a smith. He was massive; he looked like he could take the building apart by pulling the pegs out with his bare hands and then breaking the beams in half across his thigh. Furthermore, the expression on his face suggested that he was only seconds away from making the decision to begin this very renovation project.

"Batson!" The Captain looked at me. "Finally! Your duty is that you instantly leave these premises and find and retrieve Able Seaman Donald Driver. Bring him immediately to my cabin, er, office. Here. To this place."

I had never seen the Captain so flustered. Whatever was happening here was worse than being repeatedly raked by a French corvette, being almost awash in a gale storm off the Canaries, or finding oneself without a pistol in a public house full of Spaniards; all things I had survived at Captain Griffin's side. In each of those occasions, the man had never blinked an eye but today he was positively stuttering.

"Capt'in," spoke up the large man standing behind the desk, "I'd take it as a kindness toward me and me daughter if ye'd ask this feller to be quiet about what ye've asked 'im to do."

"I assure you, Mr. Black, my yeoman will act with the utmost discretion in this distasteful affair, er, that is to say, incident. I can also assure that I will see Driver hung from the nearest yardarm! To take a woman against her will, only the lowest of the . . ."

At that moment, I gasped, the girl started crying noisily, and her father let out a "Capt'in!" while eyeing me.

"Please, Capt'in Griffin," said the large man, "Give a thought, sir, to Catherine's good name!"

"I beg your forgiveness, I spoke in haste," bowed Captain Griffin. "Be on your way, Mr. Batson, and don't forget my orders."

I knew Donny Driver; I could not believe that he could do such a thing. I also knew Captain Griffin and I was sure that if he believed this girl then Donny was as good as dancing the hempen jig, as the men say. But as the Captain's yeoman, it was my duty to go and find Donny and bring him back to the Captain's onshore office. I said, "Aye, aye, Sir," did an about face and grabbed my hat as I ran by my writing desk.

I had a feeling that I knew right where Donny was. He had taken me to this place on two occasions last summer when we had returned to port for provisions, powder and ball. Donny would be at his sister's townhouse not a cable from the wharfhouse where the *Adventure* was docked and where the Captain now sat pondering the fate that would bring one of his seaman to be accused, and possibly guilty, of rape.

Captain Griffin, and his rather unusual guests, wouldn't expect me to return for an hour or more as I searched for Donny and did whatever was necessary to bring him back to face these charges. I knew I had time enough for one side trip. I was deathly afraid of what might happen to Donny and there was only one man I knew that could help me, and him, in this situation. I had met this individual about a year earlier when I was studying the Bible with the intention of becoming a man of the cloth, a destiny which I eventually avoided. I was sitting on a bench outside of a small book shop on Ratcliffe Highway, where I had just purchased a rather old and tattered Bible. I suddenly realized that there was someone standing behind the bench, obviously reading over my shoulder. I looked up and . . .

"I doubt very strenuously that you would enjoy a life spent within the Church, young man. I am sure you would much prefer a life at sea."

This was my first meeting with John Neligan, a man who would come to have a profound effect upon my life. When I first met him, he struck me as a mediumly-placed gentleman, dressed in well-fitting, though somewhat worn, breeches and hose with a coat and waistcoat of a handsome, though plain, brown color. His head was unadorned at the time, without hat or wig, and I thought he might have been a merchant who had just stepped out of his shop for a breath of fresh air.

"How did you know . . .?"

"It is the middle of the afternoon on a Tuesday; the sun is shining and the weather is beyond fair; and you are sitting on a bench reading the Good Book with the look on your face of a man trying to decide whether to have an aching tooth pulled. You are too young to be a parson and too old to be a school child. And" he said sitting down next to me, "it seemed like the best guess."

"Well, Sir, you happen to be correct but I don't know why you would disparage my goal when you do not even know me."

"My thought was born from your 'aching tooth' look, my young friend. I have nothing against preachers of the Word but I believe if yours was a true calling you might have a more serene look about you."

At this I had to chuckle and my small laugh brought a smile to his lips. He was the sort of man that looked better smiling and who you wanted to make smile. He reminded me of a headmaster of a school I attended when I was young; when he was smiling, the world could be at ease.

"Well then," I said, closing the Bible in my lap, "Why do you believe that I would be better off devoting my life to the sea?"

"Ah! In the first place, your shoes. I can see from the pattern of wear that these are the shoes that you, most likely, wear every day. They show the signs of walking on cobblestones and hard surfaces. Those scuff marks and the fact that your heels are almost as level as my reasoning. From that, I conclude that you are a city dweller, rather than the son of a tiller of the soil.

"Secondly, you can read. That suggests that you grew up in a more urban setting than a child of the fields who would, of necessity, be required to work alongside his family instead of having the opportunity of education. The fact that you had some form of education provides for a more fertile medium for an imagination. Also, growing up in a city exposes you to a more world-traveled populace and might make you wonder more about the qualities of places other than your native shores.

"And, finally," and here his own face took on an almost haunted look, "I find that there is no life better than a life at sea."

He paused, looking off into the distance, his voice trailing off into the clutter of sound that is always found along the Ratcliffe Highway. Even with the noise of the horses and wagons and the myriad cries of the vendors, his sigh was audible.

"Well, my young friend," he said after a pause, "shall we venture up to the Town of Ramsgate and I shall be more than happy to let you stand me a pint or two in repayment for this fair share of advice! I hope ye saved a few coppers from the purchase of your Bible!"

This was my introduction to Mr. Neligan. Since then, I had come to know him as a genius in most anything I ever asked. We spent many a night discussing everything from the Ark of the Covenant and its storied place in history to the signs of the zodiac and how the study of the generalizations that form the basis for this mystical circle truly can provide insight into a person's character.

Mr. Neligan was, without a doubt, the most intelligent, learned and wise individual I have ever known. He was also a drunk and a vagrant. In the nineteen months that I had known him I had never seen him perform an honest day's work. I had never seen his home and I never knew whether he lived indoors or out. His clothes were always threadbare but clean; his personal hygiene was on a par with a laborer. He shaved every few days and seemed to find the wherewithal to bath from time to time. By midnight of most nights, however, and I was witness to this on many an occasion, he would be almost catatonic with drink. Somehow, as the night wore on, he would always contrive to slink off into the night before I could follow him.

Often, I had invited him to my own lodgings and he would usually accept. But he never overstayed his welcome and, after a long day of my own employment, I would arrive home to an immaculately cleaned apartment and a cunningly wrought dinner made from whatever Mr. Neligan could find around my home. We once had a wonderful soup he made from nothing but an onion, some scraps of bread, and a lump of cheese.

On this terrible day, when I knew that my duty was to find Donny Driver and bring him back to face the Captain's wrath, I also knew where I would most likely find Mr. Neligan and I hoped that at this time of day he would still be in shape to help me. If there was any person in the world who could assist Donny it was John Neligan, presently sitting with a drink in front of him at Devil's Tavern.

Devil's Tavern was down by the docks, close to Wapping Stairs, and anyone who knows this part of the world knows that it is a place full of smugglers and pirates, cutthroats and thieves, and women of low virtue and drunkards. But it is also a place where Mr. Neligan sat like Solomon, acknowledged as the wisest of the wise and arbiter of disputes among the patrons of one of the roughest public houses in England. As shady as the place was, however, I never felt in any danger because all there knew I was a friend of Mr. Neligan.

I had been sitting by his side just two nights previous when he displayed another example of his amazing intellect and one of the few ways that I had ever seen him earn a copper or two. Two of the denizens of the Tavern had approached him with a wager about the order of the Kings of France. I suppose he could have been lying but Mr. Neligan's answer satisfied them both and earned him a portion of the sum that had been bet!

As I entered the dark pub on this day, I was acknowledged by several of the patrons and, when I asked, Mr. Neligan's whereabouts were quickly made known to me. As I had thought, he was sitting at a table near the back of the pub, alone at the moment, except for a bottle and a glass. What he was drinking I could not tell because of the lack of light in the place.

"Mr. Neligan," I asked in a hushed voice as I sat down at his table, "how is it with you today, sir?"

It was fairly early in the day but I had known Mr. Neligan to drink for thirty-six hours straight and I was somewhat afraid that I might find him drunk. He looked up as I approached.

"Ah, Jimmy Batson!" he said happily, "my young friend. How are you getting along with Captain Griffin and the *Adventure*?"

That's another piece of the story, one I shall tell someday. It was Mr. Neligan who had helped me get my employment as Captain Griffin's clark. Suffice it to say that the nature and tone of his greeting was enough to confirm to me that he was not too far gone in his daily "employment."

"Oh, I am very much satisfied with my living, thank you for asking, sir; we only just last month returned from a voyage down to the Mediterranean where I saw Gibraltar again. We continued on to Malta where I was able to see the beautiful city of Valletta."

"Ah, nothing is more well known than the siege of Malta," sighed Mr. Neligan. "You didn't look for eels in the wells, did you?"

"What, sir?"

"Nothing, lad," Mr. Neligan laughed softly, "I'm only jesting with you. But, come, there must be some reason you are here in the middle of the day. What has brought you away from your papers?"

"It's something terrible, Mr. Neligan! My friend, Donny Driver, he's been accused of attacking a young woman and I fear for his life. Captain Griffin has sent me to find him and bring him to the wharfhouse office. The girl and her father are there now! If Captain Griffin takes the girl's word against Donny's then he'll hang him! Oh, please, Mr. Neligan, you can do something to help him can't you?"

He put his hand on my shoulder and looked intently at the worry on my face. He was obviously concerned over my fear.

"I'll do what I can, lad, but don't expect miracles of me. The Good Lord gave me a few talents but He is the only one who can walk on water that I know of. Come! Let's find your friend and clear up this mess."

As we left, Mr. Neligan stopped for a few seconds to speak with the barman. He passed him a few coins and we were out the door. I told Mr. Neligan all of what I knew about the matter. He asked me some questions about Donny and he asked me to describe the girl and her father. I did the best I could but I wasn't sure if I had helped or not.

Sure enough, Donny was at his sister's home. Mr. Neligan insisted on waiting outside while I went in and spoke with Donny and his sister. I told them, per Mr. Neligan's instructions, only that Donny was urgently needed back at the ship's offices and that the Captain had instructed us to return immediately. We left Donny's sister with a worried look on her face but not half so worried as she might have been.

When we met up with Mr. Neligan outside, I let him do all the talking. He quickly and straightforwardly told Donny about the allegation. Donny's shocked reaction was enough to convince me of his innocence but I was, admittedly, a biased jury.

Mr. Neligan actually asked Donny if he would prefer to attempt to escape the charge by fleeing from the city. I can't say whether I admired him for that or not but I suppose it was further evidence of his lack of guilt when Donny said, "No, sir; it be me duty to appear and answer this charge. I can only hope that the girl be mistaken or that someone else gave her my name for her to use. Runnin' ain't for me."

I have always been envious of Donny. He was handsome, without a doubt, as fine looking a young man as I ever knew. He was tall, over six feet, and his years at sea had left him an excellent physical specimen without an ounce of fat and a ton of muscle. He was in the prime of his youth and it showed in his manner and his stride. The pall that this tragedy brought over him thankfully took the spring out of his step, otherwise I never would have been able to keep up with him.

"Alright then, let's talk as we walk. The sooner 'tis done the better is my way," said Mr. Neligan. We immediately stepped out towards the wharfhouse.

"Now then, lad, do you know this girl that has accused you? Her name, from what Jimmy has told me, is Catherine Black."

"The name does sound familiar, sir," said Donny, obviously concentrating his thoughts to try and ferret out a memory. "If I not be mistaken, she was a girl that lived near me mum and dad's place, back when I were only a lad. I never really knew 'er, she were naught but a little child of seven or eight when I were thirteen or more. If I recall 'er right, she never even paid me much mind, always lookin' down when I walked by or saw 'er lookin' out the window of her 'ouse."

"I see," said Mr. Neligan, "Very illuminating. And how long have you been at sea?"

"Well," answered Donny, "I first shipped out as an apprentice seaman when I was fifteen. I was a late bloomer, as they say. Me Dad wanted me to work in 'is cooper shop for a few years but 'e could tell that I wanted more. 'E used to share a pint or two with one of the mates of the *Phoenix* and 'e got me a berth there and me little brother, Dennis, took me place at the shop."

"I know the *Phoenix*," said Mr. Neligan. "She's a clean two-masted merchant brig. I wager you spent some time down in the Caribbean and even farther south."

"Aye, we did! We even made it 'round the Cape and . . ." Here, Donny trailed off as he spoke and he looked down at the ground as we walked.

"I'm sure you did, young man," smiled Mr. Neligan, "Did you ever make port in Madagascar?"

Donny quickly glanced up at Mr. Neligan. "Aye, we did."

"For delivery of goods, I imagine, at least when we weren't at war with the French. Did you ever manage much shore leave there?"

"Aye, sir, I did . . . ," Donny hesitated. "Why do ye ask?"

"Oh, no real reason, Donny," answered Mr. Neligan, "I just want to get a better idea of where you've sailed and with what ship. For instance, if you've sailed round the Cape of Good Hope then I know that you've crossed the equator several times."

"Oh, aye, sir, that I have! It's been years since me pollywog days!"

"Ah, a loyal member of the Court of Neptune, I see!"

"Well, no sir, just a Son of Neptune, but . . ."

"Oh, yes! Of course," said Mr. Neligan, "I recall the protocols now!"

I glanced over at Mr. Neligan and there was a knowing smile playing about his lips. I had no idea what was in his mind but for some reason I actually felt that Donny had a chance. We continued our walk, Mr. Neligan keeping up a running conversation with Donny the whole time. I couldn't help thinking the steady line of questions must surely be keeping Donny from dwelling on our final destination and the potential fate to which he was heading.

We arrived at the wharfhouse shortly before closing time for most of the local business establishments. Mr. Neligan hustled into the front door, seeming to be in a hurry. As we came to the door of the Captain's office, Mr. Neligan turned to Donny.

"You stay out here, m'lad, we'll call you in if necessary."

As we crossed the threshold of his office, Captain Griffin came to his feet, swiftly followed by Mr. Black.

"See here, Batson, I ordered you to bring back Seaman Driver! Who is this gentleman that you've brought instead."

"Captain Griffin," said Mr. Neligan taking over my turn of the wheel, "My name is Doctor Jonathan Neligan; if you will call for your First Mate, Andrew Fielding, he will vouch for my credentials. Andrew and I have been friends for a number of years, even sailing together back on the old *Lion* before she was sold out of His Majesty's Navy. You might recall her captain, Sir William Scaldron?"

"You knew, Sir William?" asked Captain Griffin, somewhat surprised.

"Aye, sir, I did. And an iron hand he was, sir! I was with the ship as surgeon when we took the *Olifant*."

"Well, sir," said Captain Griffin, smiling, and coming forward to shake "Dr." Neligan's hand. "I've heard accounts of that battle for years but I never thought to meet a veteran of that engagement! But, what brings you here on this day of all days?"

"Oh, well, I am a true friend of your yeoman here, Mr. Batson. I was out for a bite to eat from my practice when I found him, miserable, searching the streets for this Donald Driver. He was striving mightily to perform your assigned duty, sir, I tell you, and he was almost in tears of frustration! Suffice it to say, I immediately offered my assistance and not only did we find this Seaman Driver but brought him here! I also, completely against his will I might add, weaseled, as they say, the purpose of Mr. Batson's quest from him, and . . . you must be the father of this poor girl, are you not?"

Mr. Neligan quickly stepped over to Mr. Black, taking up the man's right hand in both of his, in a scene of impressive, if not commanding, sympathy.

"Oh, sir, you and your daughter have my deepest sympathies," he said, shaking Mr. Black's hand solemnly. "As a father myself, I cannot imagine what you, and she, have been put through!"

"Aye, well, . . . it's been very upsetting, to be sure . . . and I . . . thank ye for your concern." Mr. Black looked like a man who was being offered a jack of fine stout in one hand and a poisonous asp in the other. In a word, confused.

"Of course, as soon as I got it out of Jimmy what was going on I knew that I could do nothing less than come here and offer my services as a doctor to make sure that your daughter has not been, in any way endangered, by this terrible event."

At the mention of Mr. Black's daughter, all eyes turned to the young woman sitting behind the desk. This was, for the first time, my chance to take a good look at her. She had stopped crying but her eyes were still puffy and red. Even under these circumstances, I could tell that Catherine Black was pretty. Or perhaps I should say beautiful.

Her long blonde hair, disheveled as it was, combined with her sultry eyes and otherwise tawny complexion, made my mind run to those dreams we men sometimes have of tumbling between the sheets with a woman who is more wanton than we could ever imagine ourselves to be. Her clothes were nondescript and sitting down as she was I could not say if her form was pleasing or not but, watching her look back at us, biting her lower lip between her perfect white teeth, I imagined her sublimely shaped for all things prurient.

I was brought out of my aroused reverie when Mr. Neligan shouted, in a rather convincing imitation of Captain Griffin's tone, if not his voice: "Batson! Quickly! Secure paper, pen and ink! I will require you to take down all that is said here so that it can be supplied to the King's men in the impending case against Driver."

I hastened to the Captain's desk, which brought me into closer proximity to Miss Black. While I took paper, pen and ink from the Captain's supplies I was able to confirm that, at least in regard to her upper torso, Miss Black was as I have previously described her. Not only that, her cheek bones and full lips would, no doubt, have tempted St. Peter with their classical beauty, fullness and sensuality.

58

"Sit, Batson, and prepare to write!"

Mr. Neligan had taken complete control of the room. The Captain, Mr. Black and Miss Black all seemed to be shocked into silence by his tempest of action.

"Now, then, Miss Black, are you in any way hurt? Have you any bruises or cuts that you are aware of?"

For the first time, this sister to Venus spoke: "No, sir, none that I can tell."

Her voice, throaty and soft at the same time, matched her outward look.

"Well, it may be that your injuries are unknown to you because of the shock inherent in this savage attack. Pray, please forgive my indelicacy, but it is necessary for your treatment," here Mr. Neligan shot a sympathetic look at Mr. Black, "but are you, at all, bleeding, either from the physical attack or the indecencies that you suffered?"

"No . . . uh, no, sir."

"Ah! That's good, Miss Black," Mr. Neligan looked over at Mr. Black in relief, "You may have escaped the worst, even yet! Now, I only have a few more questions. It is important that I take as thorough a history as possible without causing you more distress or embarrassment."

Mr. Neligan's voice and demeanor were kind, even tender, in the delivery of these next few questions.

"Miss Black, I must ask, in as much detail as I can, for you to tell me how this event occurred."

Mr. Black started to rise form his chair, "Now, one minute 'ere, doctor . . ."

"I shall not, of course, ask you for any details of the actual assault," Mr. Neligan addressed this remark more to Mr. Black than to Miss Black but he then immediately turned back to the 'patient.' "But I must know what happened before the attack so that I can ascertain the extent of your physical injuries. So, what were you doing prior to the assault?"

"Well," Miss Black began hesitantly, "I were doing the washing, in the yard back of our place. Pa was up at the smithy, 'ere, close to town (score one for Batson, I knew he was a blacksmith!). He leaves me 'ome alone now that I turned sixteen. With Ma gone on to her reward, I do the chores 'round the 'ouse and the cooking and such."

"And so you were alone today?" Mr. Neligan asked.

"Yes, sir, I had cleaned up after the breakfast, Pa had gone to work, and I was going to finish up the washing and 'ang it up in the yard."

"I assume that your father works a regular day's work, so others must have known that you would be alone for a goodly part of the day, would that be correct?"

"Why, yes, sir. There must have been lots of people that knew that I would be alone for 'ours during the day. And what with us moving out to the county lane when Ma died, they would know that I was alone _and_ far from 'elp!"

"Do you think this Donald Driver would have had such knowledge? Have you ever met him before?"

"Oh, sir! We used to live not far from where Donny Driver lived! Now that I think on it, 'e used to look at me out of the corner of 'is eye. I used to wonder if 'e fancied me! I bet 'e came 'ome from 'is last voyage and asked after me!" She turned to her father. "That's the way, Dad, that 'e found out that I lived out of town these days and that you work late, often into the wee hours of the night! 'E must have figured 'e'd 'ave 'ours to 'ave 'is way with me!"

"Now, now, Miss Black, calm down. Please don't become overwrought. Let's take this one step at a time. That's always the best way in any criminal case."

"'Ere now," spoke up Mr. Black, "I thought you said you were a doctor? You're sounding more like a barrister with these 'ere questions."

"Well, truth be told, Mr. Black, I have served as a lay magistrate in my younger days. I find that now I prefer healing the sick to judging the guilty. But, let's get back to what happened, Miss Black. How did Driver make himself known to you?"

"Well, 'e came up to our fence, you see, and 'e began making fancy talk with me. 'E was nice and all at first, even polite. 'E came into our yard to get a ladle from the well, or so 'e said. After a bit, 'e asked me 'ow much it would be to wash 'is shirt. Well, I told 'im that I was no washerwoman and that 'e could take his trade elsewhere if that was what 'e wanted!"

"Well said, Miss Black!" Mr. Neligan interjected, sounding proud of the young girl's treatment of the accused, "The audacity of this young ruffian!"

"Oh, it got worse!" said Miss Black, warming to her tale. "We was all alone, we were, and 'e knew it! 'E slipped 'is shirt off and 'eld it out to me, strutting around trying to impress me with 'is muscles 'e was!"

"I cannot imagine what you were going through, watching this spectacle! But," said Mr. Neligan as if he had just thought of something, "This might be a boon in disguise. We have no way of knowing if Driver will try to deny this incident or not. It would be most beneficial to our case against him if you could, without going into anything more embarrassing, describe the young man's body so that perfect identification can be made. What time of day was it when this occurred?"

"Oh!" said Miss Black conspiratorially, "I see. Well, it was perhaps the middle of the morning. I know it couldn't 'ave been later because what saved me was Pa coming up, unexpected like, for the noon meal."

"Excellent! So, as he was prancing shirtless in the yard, there must have been plenty of light to see his rude and offensive display!"

"Well, yes, sir, there was . . . but I don't know what you might mean about describing 'is body."

"Hmm, let's see if we can make it easy, shall we?" said Mr. Neligan. "Did he have any noticeable scars or birthmarks or tattoos or any such marking on his chest or upper body?"

"Well, none that I could see, but his chest was all-covered with 'air, so there might 'ave been something and I just didn't see it."

"Now look 'ere," interjected Mr. Black, "This is all a great deal of talking about something that's fair easy to see. This bloody sailor came into my yard, took advantage of my daughter's being alone and out from town. When she wouldn't do what 'e wanted, 'e dragged 'er inside our 'ouse, knowing I would be in town working at the smithy, forced 'er into 'er bedroom and 'ad 'is way with 'er on 'er bed. That's where I found 'er, 'alf-naked and screaming, 'get out, get out' and 'im through the window before I could get full into the room."

"So you were not able to get a good look at the wrongdoer?" asked Mr. Neligan.

"No," said Mr. Black, obviously frustrated by the interminable questioning, "but I don't know what difference that . . ."

As Mr. Black was speaking, Mr. Neligan walked to the door of the Captain's office.

"Step in, Mr. Driver, if you please," said Mr. Neligan.

"Now see 'ere!" started Mr. Black.

"We'll all see momentarily, my good man! I promise you that absolutely no harm will come to your daughter! Young Batson there will restrain him or you yourself can arrest him if he in any way seeks to offend your daughter."

Once again, through the use of his voice and, what had become, his imposing presence, Mr. Neligan brought quiet to the "proceedings." If I hadn't known better I would have imagined myself back at Devil's Tavern with Mr. Neligan presiding over a dispute amongst the denizen's of that place!

"Can you identify this man, Miss Black, as the man who harmed you?"

The girl looked up at Donny and tears came into her lovely eyes. She began sobbing, looking so defenseless and grief-stricken. She sobbed into her handkerchief as she said, softly, "Yes, sir, that be Donny Driver."

At that moment, taking down the poor girl's testimony, I could almost have hung Donny myself. Mr. Neligan turned to the girl's father.

"Can you, Mr. Black, identify this man as your daughter's attacker?"

I sat with quill in hand waiting to take down the smith's next words. He looked Donny up and down.

"No," he said at last, "It's like I told ye. Poor Catherine was screaming and . . . 'e was out the window before I could get a good look at 'im! It was all I could do with Catherine nearly swooning in me arms and running out the whole story . . . she was beside 'erself, she was!"

Mr. Neligan was listening to Mr. Black, intently, when he suddenly perked up and said, "Catherine Black? Catherine Black? I wonder, Miss Black, have you ever gone by the nickname 'Cat'? Has anyone ever called you 'Cat Black'?"

At the mere mention of that name, Miss Black's countenance changed completely. She raised her head from her handkerchief and a look of venomous hatred came over her face. If I hadn't seen it myself, I would never have allowed that she could look the way she did. For an instant, it appeared as if she could have killed Mr. Neligan where he stood; if her eyes had been flintlocks, Mr. Neligan would never have seen another dawn. But, glancing sideways at her father, Miss Black just as quickly caught herself and immediately softened her look again.

"Oh, some of me girlfriends might have called me that, when we were little things, playing among our 'ouses."

Mr. Neligan stared her in the eye for a few seconds, a slow smile playing across his lips.

"Yes," he said, "I thought I might have heard that name before. Now,"turning toward Donny," as for this fellow . . ."

In two quick strides, Mr. Neligan was standing before Donny and, before anyone could react, he had reached up with both hands, thrust his fingers through Donny's open collar and ripped Donny's shirt completely open down the front.

Amidst the cries of surprise and angry remonstration for this act of rudeness, Mr. Neligan simply stood aside and let us all see Donny's bare chest. Contradicting the testimony given by Miss Black, Donny's chest was, for the most part, barren of the hairiness which she had claimed to have seen.

Not only that, but there, in plain view, even in the lower light of the office windows, covering Donny's chest was a three-masted sailing ship under full sail with waves dancing along her sides. It was, under the circumstances, the most beautiful tattoo I have ever seen!
Mr. Black took one look at the tattoo and then slowly turned his attention back to his daughter.

"Now, Pa," she said, "I can explain . . ."

The speed with which I had earlier that day flown down the corridor to the Captain's office was as a tortoise might crawl compared to the flash that was Catherine Black as she exited the room. Her father, with a look of embarrassment combined with rage, barely got out, "Sorry, Capt'in," before he strode after her with the clear intent of thrashing her into the truth. I would rather have had Cerberus on my trail at that moment than be "Cat Black."

After the moment had passed and Donny had pulled his shirt back together in some semblance of decency, the Captain looked at Mr. Neligan and said, "Doctor Neligan, that was, without a doubt, the most incredible display of legal genius that I have ever seen!"

Captain Griffin came forward and reached for Mr. Neligan's hand; as he earnestly shook it, he glanced at Donny, and said, "Thank God, the stars, and the four winds, me boy! I am delighted to have you back in good graces! But, wait a moment; do you two know each other?"

Captain Griffin was looking back and forth between the two when I stepped forward and said, "No, sir; Mist . . ., er, Doctor Neligan and I are acquainted. If you'll recall he told you so when we arrived."

"Why, yes, I do recall that now that you mention it. Pray, Doctor, how in the world did you know that Seaman Driver had a tattoo on his chest?"

Mr. Neligan was beaming. "It was nothing more than a matter of my familiarity with the ways of sailors and their travels. After Mr. Driver here had told me he had been at sea for six years, that he had crossed the line on numerous occasions, that he had sailed the waters of the Caribbean, that he had been to Madagascar and enjoyed the shore leave there, . . . well, it follows without any doubt at all that some part of him, particularly his chest, would have been painted in the manner of the Southern Seas. It seemed like the best guess. I knew that Mr. Black would never permit the demonstration that I intended, and I apologize, sir, I admit to owing you a shirt. I took matters into my own hands, so to speak."

"And what would you have done if there had been no tattoo to be seen?" asked Captain Griffin.

"Well, Captain," and here Mr. Neligan glanced at his shoes in embarrassment, "There I must ask your forgiveness and your forbearance and that you let me explain. You see, sir, I am not currently employed in the practice of medicine. I have been a ship's surgeon in the past but for a number of years now, too long for that matter, I have been adrift on a sea of a completely different sort. A few years ago, for reasons that I beg you not to inquire of, I came ashore and began a life of drunkenness. I am a regular at most every public house along the docks and have squandered my days and nights trying to lose myself and my past by drinking all manner of spirits. I have become a mere ghost of the man I once was and while there are reasons, there can be no excuse for . . ."

64

Here, Mr. Neligan drifted off into silence and simply sat staring at his hands. He could not see, as could I, the look of sympathy on Captain Griffin's face. To his eternal credit, Captain Griffin walked over to where Mr. Neligan had sat down and put his hand upon his shoulder: "My friend, I have watched as others walked the same path. Most get lost and never come back. But the man I watched today; the man who saved one of my sailors, is not a man who will lose his way easily. Whatever caused you to stumble is not for me to ask. Instead, in memory of Sir William, all I say is that if there ever be anything I can do to help, all you need do is ask."

At that moment, Mr. Neligan looked up with the light of hope in his eyes and spoke in a rush, "What I ask, Captain, is a place aboard the *Adventure* when next she sails. I'll sail as an Ordinary Seaman, if you please, whatever you choose. Just let me get back to the sea!"

A smile grew across Captain Griffin's face, and mine, as the Captain reached out his hand and said, "With pleasure, Doctor, I mean, Mr. Neligan. But," he spoke as if he'd thought better of his offer, "only on one condition – you never answered my question. What would you have done if there had been no tattoo aboard Mr. Driver's chest?"

"Oh, well," said Mr. Neligan with a redness to his face, "As I said, sir, Mr. Driver wouldn't have been much of a sailor without some spot of paint about him. In the same way, I wouldn't have been much of a drunkard without having seen and heard of Cat Black! She's well known among the public houses as a woman of ill repute and, while I have never availed myself of her favors, I know her by sight. You could see how she reacted when I mentioned her nickname; can you imagine what she would have done if I'd brought in a few of her clientele?"

At this we all, even Donny, burst into laughter. I could well imagine the scene that would have ensued and I think we all had a good idea of how Mr. Black would have reacted.

"Batson! You scurvy dog," Captain Griffin cried good naturedly, "Get out the log book! Let's sign Mr. Neligan aboard!"

"Aye, Captain!"

I stepped to the Captain's desk and reached into the drawer where I knew the log of the *Adventure* rested and brought it out. Opening it on the desk, I readied pen and ink and prepared to log Mr. Neligan in as a member of the crew. Reaching out his hand, he stopped me and looked with some seriousness at Captain Griffin.

"Captain, if I am to be a member of your crew," Mr. Neligan said, "then I must sign in with my true name."

I almost gasped. Ever since I had known this man, for almost two years, I had always called him "John Neligan." It appeared this day that there was no end to his revelations!

"My true name," he said taking the pen, "The name that I was born with is . . ."

Ghost Of The Sea

Halfway down the path everything disappears,
All the light and joy of my youthful years.
Friend, neighbor, and foe.
All seems to drift with tide's ebb and flow.
Until I could only see,
But a few feet in front of me.
Not a soul in sight,
Solitude keeps me company tonight.

Nothing is what it may seem,
Like being caught in a net called "Dream."
Where truth is untrue; and all that lies,
Is right there in front of your very eyes.
That is where I want to be,
Somewhere between the harbor and the sea.
That place where all my anguish will cease,
That place where I can finally find peace.

Long is the elder woman's hair,
That did catch me unaware.
She did take me by the hand,
And I felt as though I was no longer on land.
Fog, and sea are not in part, but whole.
With her tighten coif she pulled me below.
As I walked the underwater shore,
I realized I had been here long before.

I belonged to her, and she to the sea.
A ghost within a ghost, for all eternity!

                    Shana L. Martin
                    ©2009
                    Inspired by: God, and "Long Day's Journey into Night"
                    By Eugene O'Neill

The Scottish Pirate

I left my Highland home

       To sail across the sea

The king took my religion

       No more can I be free

They say I am an outlaw

       Not fit to own my turf

So now I sail across the sea

       And watch unnatural surf

It seems I have no country

       No more can I go home

I have to live among the waves

       Among the briny foam

With my plaid wrapped all around me

       I raise the bones and skull

And fire my cannons loud and clear

       To bore into your hull

And you, oh English Navy

       Commissioned by the king

You'll see my flag of black

       And hear my cutlass ring

You took away my country

    My religion and much more

And I will see you go to hell

    Upon the ocean floor

You once called me an outlaw

    Well, outlaw I became

And well before I see the Lord

    You'll bow before my name

You cannot treat my kinsmen such

    And expect them all to not

Retaliate in such a way

    My God, man, I'm a Scot

    Pamala A. Williams
    ©2009

The Pirate Christmas Party
(With apologies to Robert Louis Stevenson, Young E. Allison, and pirates everywhere!)

Fifteen men 'round the Christmas tree,
Ho, ho, ho, and a bottle of rum!
All were pirates including me.
Ho, ho, ho, and a bottle of rum.
The party was loud and runnin' wild,
Celebratin' the birth of the dear Christ child,
But this were no place for the meek or mild!
There was meat and drink for all to spare,
The table was laden with Christmas fare
And red and green rigging for all to wear!
Ho, ho, ho, and a bottle of rum.

Fifteen men with presents for all,
Ho, ho, ho, and a bottle of rum.
Some were great and some were small.
Ho, ho, ho, and a bottle of rum
The cap'n brought a brand new blade,
The mate he brought some socks he made,
The bosun brought silk of ruby shade.
All went under the Christmas tree,
Boxed or bagged so none could see,
While the crew carried on the festivity!
Ho, ho, ho, and a bottle of rum!

Fifteen gifts for the pirates and tars,
Ho, ho, ho, and a bottle of rum,
Some in boxes and some in jars.
Ho, ho, ho, and a bottle of rum
Cookie boiled some special sweets,
Bucky broiled some smoky meats,
Each gob they brought some special treats.
And they were piled so shiny and bright,
They looked just like the stars at night,
Bound in paper and tied up tight
Ho, ho, ho, and a bottle of rum.

70

Fifteen pirates all feastin' and drinkin',
Ho, ho, ho, and a bottle of rum!
Each manjack there was sittin' and thinkin'
Ho, ho, ho and a bottle of rum!
 "Which package should I choose to pick?"
"Which of all will do the trick?"
"Will Cookie's gift there make me sick?"
Then came the time to choose a gift,
Under the tree we all did drift,
To see which present each would lift.
Ho, ho, ho, and a bottle of rum!

The good captain chose the ruby silk,
Ho, ho ho and a bottle of rum,
The mate he got some coconut milk,
Ho, ho ho and PUT IT IN THE RUM!
The bosun got the captain's blade,
Cookie got the socks handmade,
And Bucky got a ring of jade.
I wound up with the boiled sweets
And passed them out for all to eat
That way I stayed upon my feet!
Ho, ho, ho, and a bottle of rum!

Fifteen pirates loudly carols singing!
Ho, ho, ho, and a bottle of rum!
Christmas bells are merrily ringing!
Ho, ho, ho, and a bottle of rum!
The crew is like a family this night,
With food and drink we all delight,
And presents that fit us all just right
We welcome the Christ child to the Earth,
With laughter and joy and peaceful mirth
We sing His praises for all we're worth!
Ho, ho, ho, and Merry Christmas to all!!

Stephen Sanders
©2008

Tales From The Mist

Death or Glory

Under winter sky's frigid embrace, with snorting horses,
Hot breath clouding,
The armies of riders met, panoply ablaze,
Ablaze for death or glory –
For the glory of their kings.

Knee to knee, in line abreast, the lancers curbed and pranced,
The snap and flutter of guidon heard.
The clarion call to battle sounds,
Sounds for death or glory –
For the glory of their kings.

With glittering helm and seating checked, slow walk, then trot,
Sweating in the cold.
At final brassy shout, the wall of lances lowered,
Lowered for death or glory –
For the glory of their kings.

Whispering ring of metal, as steel clears scabbard's steel,
At opposite charged hussars,
Pelisses blowing, shakos tight, curved sabers raised on high,
On high for death or glory –
For the glory of l'Empereur.

With glittering points and slashing edge,
the thunder of the charge,
Till the brothers met in battle,
Battle for death or glory –
For the glory of their kings.

With gimlet eye, the sun gazed down upon the slaughter.
Rolling eyes, steaming blood,
Snapped, broken tools of war. Screams,
Screams for death or glory –
For the glory of their kings.

Death has won this battle,
Yet Glory stands beside,
For every heart beat true, and risked,
In this Death or Glory ride.
For the glory of their kings.

Keith McGraw
©2006

The Darkness
By Scott Goodrich
©2009

The Darkness filled the air. There was no sound but for the breathing, and barely that. The two opposing forces had assembled on opposite sides of the battlefield early, before dawn, that fateful day. Each side was poised to do their best to exterminate their foes. The night before had been stifling, burning hot, and humid, impossible for any to get descent sleep or rest before the coming battle.

Each man was anxious to be done with this battle, for the war had raged for many years now, and it seemed that each force was evenly matched to one another. The conflict had come down to this, the last battle, the last line, the last of the able fighting men, a defeat or victory for one or the other. The commanders and seconds had ridden out to meet each other in the middle of the field to discuss the terms of battle, as they had done on so many occasions before. They had lingered for a long while making each side more anxious than before. At last each side had broken off and was returning to their respective forces to give the word.

The Commander, on a stone white steed, started riding up and down the line of men standing ready. Shouting to his men that the word of battle is no quarter, leave no one alive. These orders hardened the men as the Commander passed. Bracing themselves for the inevitable, they let their rage and primal instincts take over. The Commander came riding back by and ordered the men to ready themselves for battle.

The cold, shivering ring of steel being drawn and presented pierced the air and rang out across the battlefield, and as in answer the opposing force did likewise. The honed edges of swords, axes, and spears were poised at the ready across the lines as the faint light of dawn started creeping across the land. Each weapon held at the ready in the hand of its wielder, some were old and worn, others were pristinely new, but all were razor sharp and ready to deal death.

Thick, piercing, beams of sunlight shot across the field as the sun crested over the horizon. The light reflected off weapons all across the lines, sending blades of light here and there blinding some momentarily in a mocking attempt to gain an advantage. The horns of battle sounded across the field, and the men stood ready, waiting for the next sound. The second blast of the horns pierced the air and hell was unleashed upon the field. Each force surged toward the other as if a dam had burst forth with a tidal wave of water, only it was men that poured over the land in a cacophony of screaming and shouting.

Time seemed to slow to a crawl as the forces rushed to meet each other but, before they could, something stirred in the middle of the field. Something otherworldly and unseen began moving through the oncoming horde of attackers, cutting them down as they came, fluidly moving back and forth in a dance of death and carnage. No one was the wiser as the unseen thing hacked and sliced its way through the men. It was everywhere and nowhere. You could only see where it had been from the lifeless corpses it left in its wake. The haze and blur of motion from the thing and the forces doing battle was mesmerizing. In the commotion you could barely make out a double headed axe swinging about, whistling through the air creating a song of destruction as it cleaved through muscle and bone leaving a path of death in its wake.

It moved about, dodging, ducking, swinging the axe back and forth, round and round, whistling, cutting, and cleaving, truly a definitive sight of pure unhindered death. The sounds of death rang out all around as the slaughter ensued. The wailing, and screams of the dying, rose and fell in the air like a chorus of the dammed being dragged off to hell. As the symphony of death continued, a wave of fear and terror spread throughout the field, some stood their ground only to be cut down like so much wheat in the fields; others were struck down from behind in a futile attempt to escape the raging carnage moving about the battlefield.

There was no escape for any as all were here to die one way or another. The forces of both sides, even with the overwhelming numbers, were just waiting in line for the death that was inevitable. The realization of their predicament became all too clear as the horror mounted and the death toll rose with each passing second. It was happening so fast as if death himself was waving his hand across the minions, cutting them down as easily as one might take a breath of air.

Time seemed to regain itself and start again; a breeze trickled across the field as the sun continued its journey up into the sky. The smell of death and decay hung in the air. It was only the lack of foes and the silence of the dead that made the thing stop. Death was everywhere, bodies all about, piled atop each other and strewn around as if tossed like so much garbage and debris. A veritable sea of flesh stretched as far as one could see. Men, young and old, high ranking and lowly ground fodder alike had all met the same fate on the field of battle.

Amidst the rising stink and haze, you could hear the carrion and vermin calling out an invitation to their brethren, for a feast of flesh; to come and partake of the succulent buffet left for them. Come they did, one and all. Rats and Vultures were the first to arrive, wringing their paws and, salivating at the spread before them. Others took their time, ants and worms and such, for they knew there was plenty for all.

The axe swung up one final time to rest upon the things' shoulder, making a heavy thunking sound as it rested into place. The handle, warm from friction, steamed in the morning air as the blade was cooling from its death dealing flight.

Primordial ooze glistened and fell from the blade giving the axe and handle a glow that seemed to shimmered with a life of its own. After a few moments the figure stood tall and stretched as the sun rose higher into the sky. The axe shone brightly, as the sun gleamed off of it as it sat there on the Things shoulder, the Thing that had come and laid waste to the tens of thousands of men that had come to do battle. The Thing looked out across the field, surveying the carnage it had wrought. Looking to make sure it had done its deed to the fullest, watching and waiting for any to stir, for any signs that it may have missed that one important soul, but nothing moved but the carrion. It had done its job too well.

The Thing finally satisfied that it was over, pulled a parchment from its vestments, unrolled it and regarded it for a time. It then pulled a feather pen, and made some marks on the parchment. It unrolled the parchment farther, nodded its head and then returned the parchment and pen from where they were taken. Slowly the thing turned towards a new direction. Slowly and methodically it made its way through the field of the dead. The carrion and vermin made a path so it could pass easily, not out of respect but out of courtesy for the meal it had provided. As the Thing passed, the path was reclaimed, and the buffet continued. It would last for days, even weeks as they did their work to rid the world of the evidence left behind of such a conflict.

As the Thing moved off to some other place in the distance, the Lifeless corpses lay twisted and mangled, strewn about the field. Some piled on top of one another, some lying alone by themselves, but all had looks of terror and fear burned into their faces. Only the vermin and insects moved about the field, happily feasting upon the dead in a vicious cycle of life and death. Only on closer inspection of the dead would anyone notice that there was not a drop of blood anywhere or on anything.

The Axe, the axe of death was not forged for trivial battle of normal means. No; it was made for one special purpose alone. In the carnage on the field the axe never tore through flesh and bone, but cut much deeper than anything could. It cut clear to the soul, and sucked out the life of all that it touched and sent it screaming and howling off to hell. There to be tormented and forced into the ever growing army of the dead.

The Thing, not looking back nor caring what it left behind moved off into the mountains. A slow wailing began to rise from the axe, as if it was pining or anxious for the next conflict or battle to begin so it could be about doing its deathly duties. Soon the wailing changed to a symphony of crooning and moaning as it celebrated the souls and the work it had done this day, rising into a song of woe, torment, and expectations as Death moved on to another appointment.

POISONED
By Pamala A. Williams
©2009

"Strayla," Reinholt hurried to his love. "Strayla, the master has left us some food."

Strayla stopped placing the rags for their bedding as she looked at him in amazement.

"That is impossible. The master does not even know we are here. Why would he leave food for us?"

"Strayla," Reinholt said condescendingly. "He is a compassionate man. Does he not leave food for the hound? And of course he would know we are here. He is the master of the house. He knows the winter is coming soon. He knows that those of us who are without would take refuge in his great house. How could he not know? It is very hard on us with the weather turning so cold. And with the little ones coming," he looked at Strayla's bulging figure, "we need all the help we can get. I'm sure he is being kind."

Strayla straightened. It was close to her time. The babies would be here any day. The food would be nice. It was getting more and more difficult to forage for food as winter bore down. As her stomach chose that particular moment to growl, she made up her mind. With a nod she said, "Show me this food."

Reinholt led her to a container that had been put out for them. Food. True, it was not what they were used to, but it was nourishment. Reinholt worried so much about Strayla. The pregnancy was taking its toll. She seemed to have little energy as her time came close. Soon, they would have a family. He was both excited at the prospect, and worried. But with the master of the house taking care of them this winter, he was sure that he would be able to provide for them once spring came. With food growing in the fields, life would be easier on them.

Strayla and Reinholt ate their fill. It was so good to finally have full bellies. They made their way back to their hidden chamber. Now was a good time for sleep.

*   *   *   *   *

79

"Reinholt!" Strayla screamed. Reinholt came awake in a flash.

"Strayla, my love, what is wrong?" He stared at her. "Is it time? Are the babies coming?"

Strayla turned tear streaked eyes to the one she loved. She doubled over as pain wracked her body. "No, Reinholt. We must flee. We must get away. The master has poisoned us. We must find water. Perhaps water will dilute the poison."

It was then that Reinholt felt his body jolt with pain. Poison. No. It couldn't be. The master of the house was kind and benevolent. Why would he poison them?

Reinholt and Strayla ran. They had to find water. They had to try something.

Strayla screamed and collapsed. Reinholt, pain infusing his body, wrapped himself close to her. If they had to die, they would die together.

"Strayla," he gasped, "always remember that I love you."

*   *   *   *   *

"There they are," said Sebastian. "I knew there had to be one somewhere. But two. Now that is something."

Sebastian looked at the two bodies curled up beside each other. He shook his head.

"I hate rats. Glad these two are gone." He picked up the bodies by their long nude tails and dumped them unceremoniously into a plastic trash bag. He looked down at his prancing dog.

"Well, Buddy, let's see if we can find out where they came in and plug up the hole. Don't want any more rats in here. Probably wouldn't hurt to put out more rat poison, just in case."

Liberator Village
By Stephen Sanders
©2009

For the umpteenth time, Billy "Badass" Barnes watched the old guy shuffle down the street carrying two plastic shopping bags from the FineMart on Cherry Lane. The ancient fart looked like he was old enough to have fought in the Revolutionary War (whenever that was) and he looked feeble enough that losing one of the bags that he was carrying would tip him over like a bicycle without a kick stand. Billy laughed the first few times he had seen the old guy. Even now, thinking about running down to the street and pulling one of the bags from the guy's hands just to see if he would fall over, made Billy laugh till he almost peed his jeans.

But what drove "Badass" really crazy about the whole thing was wondering why in the hell the old shithead didn't just drive down to the FineMart. The old man had made this trip almost daily for the last couple of months and it looked like he was going to drop dead every time he went. It was the middle of summer in central Texas and the temperature had to be getting close to 101, but the old guy got out just about every day around two in the afternoon and walked down to the FineMart, bought God-knew-what, and walked back. The trip was easily a mile each way. Billy never would have walked it if he was the old guy, especially not when the old fucker had such a tight ride sitting in his driveway.

Billy didn't know diddlysquat about old cars but he knew that this one was not only worth some money it was also one of the finest cars Billy had ever seen in his life. It was red and white and had fins that ran down the back and ended in red taillights that looked like something off of a space ship. When the old guy drove it, and Billy noticed him driving it only on the weekends, the motor sounded like Billy felt when he had been beating up one of his many victims in high school - tough and cool and horny and mad and clear-headed; all of it, all at the same time. The sound made Billy want to get in the car and drive it, drive it like that old fart never would.

The old man sorta stumbled. A different kind of guy might have hopped off the porch and trotted down to ask the old guy if he was all right. A different kind of neighbor might even have hopped into his old beat up Ford Ranger and asked the old man if he wanted a ride. But "Badass" Barnes was not that kind of guy at all.

*   *   *   *   *

"Badass" had been born and raised in White Settlement, Texas, a sleepy little suburb of Fort Worth. The town had once been called "Liberator Village" after the B-24 bombers manufactured during World War II at the local aircraft plant. At one time, the plant had employed over 33,000 workers and had been the largest air conditioned building in the world. Also, there had been an Air Force base next door that brought a constantly revolving population in from all over the world. The little community had ridden the tidal wave of defense spending during the Cold War and had grown to the point of booming.

Then, along came the fall of the Berlin Wall and the rounds of base closures by Congress and the boom had gone bust. The bomber plant was a third of the size it used to be and while the Air Force base was still in operation as a reserve base, it would never again be like it was when Billy had grown up there. It would never again be full of young daughters of the stiffs that worked at the plant. Young daughters that were excited by the long haired, tattooed, motorcycle rider named "Badass" Barnes that they could use to piss-off their crew cut fathers. And it would never again be full of young Airmen spending their payday nights off base who could be separated from their cash with a pool cue – either hustled or bashed, Billy didn't care.

What the town was full of now were retirees. All of the old people who had been laid off from the various aircraft manufacturers that had inhabited the plant were now trying to live out their "golden years" in the little tract houses they had bought when they went to work for Convair and General Dynamics and Lockheed Martin. Not only that, the place was full of Air Force pukes who settled in the area because they thought that the base would always be there to let them use the commissary and the BX and the big base hospital that was closed around the end of the nineties. What a joke on them! Now they were stuck in this one mule town (it didn't even deserve a horse) living on fixed incomes and trying to deal with inflation, the rising cost of medical care, and an economy that was struggling to make it around the track one more time.

Just like the old guy stumbling down the street in front of Billy's parent's old house was trying to make it one more time.

Billy lived alone in his tiny house now, his parents were dead. They had died a few years back, both from cancer. It had been lung cancer in both cases and they probably got it from smoking the same brand of cigarettes that Billy was chain-smoking now. His mom went first and she was only 56. His dad had kicked off a year later, almost to the day, and he had been 59. They had left him the crummy little house because they didn't have anything else to give him. Their savings had gone up in smoke, no pun intended, trying to pay the medical bills that two catastrophic illnesses can produce. Billy didn't give a damn, though, this place was a roof over his head and the surrounding area was, to steal a phrase, a target rich environment.

Billy had grown into a small-time crook. He had been one ever since he had graduated from high school. He had tried to go to a community college; he had wanted to be a computer programmer. But the school was hard and they didn't just move you along the way they did in public school. Billy got bored too quick and none of the girls were interested in the "bad boy" mystique that had gotten Billy so much action when he'd been seventeen. So, he gave it up. Breaking into his first house made it all very easy.

It happened almost as an accident. Billy was riding home from one of his last days at the community college on the old Harley he used to have and had stopped at a stop sign. He noticed a family leaving their house, all dressed up and looking like they were going out on the town. The lights in the house were off and the man, woman, and two boys were climbing into a minivan. They were laughing and talking, looking like the kind of family that would go out to eat and to the movies together. In an instant, Billy had made his mind up what he was going to do. He had thought about this a lot in the past and had talked about how easy it would be with some of his buddies. Now he'd find out if he had been right.

He made his turn and rode down the highway for a few miles. Then he took the next exit and looped back, driving into the same neighborhood where he'd seen the family getting into their car. It was getting dark fast and the neighborhood was full of nice, quiet homes where people sat in front of their TV's eating dinner glued to the tube. Billy figured if he didn't make a lot of noise breaking in, and there was no dog, he could ride right up into the driveway and be gone in ten or fifteen minutes.

He parked his bike right up next to the house, where he could get onto it in a hurry if he needed to and where the shadow cast by the rise in the center of the roof would cloak him completely. There were no signs out front warning of the house being protected by such-and-such alarm company so Billy stopped worrying about alarms. He made his way around to the back of the house and found a backdoor concealed from the neighbors by a privacy fence so he stopped worrying about the neighbors. He didn't hear any barking when he got up close to the door so he stopped worrying about a dog. Billy used the short tire iron he had stowed in his toolbox on the bike to pry the door open and he was in.

Straight upstairs to the bedrooms. The first one was a kid's room. Billy pulled the pillow off the bed, the cover off the pillow, and crammed about fifty CDs, DVDs and CD games into the pillowcase. He immediately moved to the next bedroom through an adjoining bathroom and discovered another kid's room. And about fifty more CDs, DVDs and CD games. They went into the pillowcase. In less than five minutes of being in the house, he had covered two bedrooms and had a nice haul going already.

Billy left the kid's room and went out into the hallway. He made a right, went past what looked like a linen closet and found that the rest of the upstairs was a big playroom – pool table, shelves with board games, and something else – an entertainment center with a TV, DVD player and a stereo. And there was some kind of game thing hooked up to the TV. Sure enough, there were more CDs in a rack by the stereo, DVDs galore and a bunch more CD games. Now, downstairs, hurry, find the parent's room.

Billy hustled downstairs and looked around real quick. The place was still as quiet as a tomb and from the light coming in the windows from outside he could see well enough to know that there no surprises waiting for him. It took him just a couple of minutes to find the parents' bedroom and he went straight to the chest of drawers that looked like it belonged to the woman. He rifled through the drawers and found a couple of boxes with jewelry in them. These he dropped into the pillowcase and noticed that the case was getting full. Damn! He was going to look like Santa Clause in September walking out of there! Oh, well, next time he'd come up with something better . . . that was the first and only time that Billy hesitated.

"Would there be a next time?" he wondered.

At that moment a slow smile spread across his lips and Billy made a decision that would change his life forever.

"Damn right there'll be a next time, this is as easy as pie," thought Billy "Badass" Barnes.

A second later, Billy made a discovery that was the icing on the cake – in the back of the closet there was a long leather case that started Billy's mouth watering. Sure enough, inside there was a shotgun of some kind. It was heavy and smelled like gun oil and Billy figured he had struck gold. It was going to be a bitch getting it home but it was worth the gamble. In another thirty seconds, Billy was out the back door and on his bike. It didn't even dawn on him until he was on his bike that the riding gloves he was wearing had taken care of whatever fingerprints he might have other wise left. He smiled again; it was like it was meant to be. If he had been caught that night, things might have been very different for Billy, but as luck would have it, Billy made it around a few corners with the sack in one hand and the front end of the leather case wedged under the muffler. He looked like some new age bandito carrying home a sack of pesos stolen from the local bank but he traveled fast and he made it to an abandoned office building that still had its dumpster. He stashed his loot, rode home lickety-split, and borrowed his dad's beat up Datsun. The old man didn't even ask him what he wanted it for. The TV was on and dinner was on the tray in front of him. "Yeah, whatever."

The next couple of days, Billy spent the time that he was supposed to be studying computers driving over to Dallas and hitting a couple of used CD and DVD stores, game stores, used book stores and pawnshops. He had walked out of those people's house with almost 120 CD's, an equal amount of DVD's and more CD games than he ever knew existed. He didn't sell more than ten at any one place and felt kind of funny when he sold some of the crap, his long hair just didn't quite fit with a Perry Como Christmas CD. But the jokers behind the counters didn't seem to care what they were buying or from who. Besides, someone was going to come in someday looking for that exact CD and would be happy to find it on the $3.99 sale rack. Hell, some people still listen to disco.

With the CDs, DVDs and games Billy averaged about a buck each. By the end of his trips to the various half-priced CD, DVD, game and book joints he was about $320 to the good. But it was the shotgun that sealed his fate. He went into a crappy looking pawnshop on the southeast side of Dallas and gave the guy a sob story about how the gun had been left to him by his father and he didn't hunt and he just didn't have any use for it but he really needed the money.

The pawnbroker's first offer was $160. By the time he left, Billy had talked the guy up to $200. Little did "Badass" know that it was an $800 Winchester that the pawnbroker knew he could unload for about $450 and that the pawnbroker had figured out he'd never see Billy again. But Billy walked out of the pawnshop over $500 richer for a couple of days work. To him, this was like finding money lying around on the ground. He had finally found a job where he could get paid for doing things he enjoyed! That three-day period changed his life forever.

From that time on, Billy worked little odd jobs from time to time. He'd flip burgers at a McDonald's until he got tired of it or stock shelves at some supermarket till he mouthed off once too often to the manager. But the purpose for these jobs was to give him his "cover" for his real profession. He even drew unemployment from time to time when he'd lose a job because he was laid off. All the time, he lived with his parents, played the role of the miserable failure of a son, and pulled off one small time job after another. He got pretty good at it after awhile and made some contacts in the "business." He even took a step up on a few occasions and burgled small businesses.

He was averaging about $900 a month from his larceny. That's not bad money when you are living for free at your parent's house and not paying taxes on your income. Billy was getting tired of the crap he was taking from his old man, though. If he'd had to live like that for too much longer he might have done something stupid – like moving out. But his luck and his lack of morals held and he continued his lifestyle and watched both of his parents die off. And that's how he wound up living in the bedroom where he was conceived.

86

"Fuck, I gotta get outta this town," Bill thought to himself, leaning forward on his knees, "If not, it ain't gonna be that long before I'm like that old bastard out there. I'll be stuck in this shithole till the day I die."

The old man stopped his shuffling and set down his packages. He reached into his back pocket and pulled out a wrinkled old handkerchief, "probably full of snot-balls," thought Billy, and the old man used the handkerchief to wipe his sweating forehead. The dude sort of turned around, standing where he was, looking up at the sun, at the houses around him, acting like he was just now figuring out that he had walked about a mile and a half in the blazing sun. His three-sixty resulted in him noticing Billy sitting up on the porch; he smiled an old man's smile and waved up to Billy. Just like he had done every time he had seen Billy sitting on the porch.

"Hot enough for ya," yelled Billy, waving back at him, and adding under his breath, "ya old fuck."

The old man laughed, a laugh that came out of his throat wet and ragged, and called back as loud as he could, "Yep; yep, sure is. Seems like it gets hotter every day now. Take care, young man, see ya down the road." With that, the old man bent painfully, picked up the plastic bags and started moving again.

"And tell me old man," Billy whispered aloud, leaning forward in his lawn chair and setting his question, on the spot, to a sing-song tune, "why ain't you driving that sweet cherry car? Is it too much for ya, huh? Can't keep it on the road like you used ta?" Billy's eyes never left the man as he continued humming his little tune; never once left the man who was going to become his latest prey.

The concept of "prey" had become very important to Billy in the last few years. He discovered that living where he did was like being a lion in the middle of a pack of zebra that were deaf, dumb and blind. He was surrounded by old people. People who retired from the GD plant or who worked for Tarrant County or who used to be civil servants out at the base before it closed. The median age of the people living around Billy was over seventy. Many of them lived alone. Some of them had been living in their own little worlds for so long that they probably wouldn't know what "911" was. And most of them were afraid – afraid of death, afraid of life, afraid of anything that would interrupt the nice little routine that they had developed for their final years.

He started dropping in on his neighbors, most of the time without their even knowing it. He would walk into their garages, take whatever he wanted and just walk home. Some of his neighbors were so lonely or so scared that they would give him things to get him to come over or to leave them alone. Either way, he made out like the bandit that he had become. And now, the old guy was going to become his next victim.

He wanted that car, he needed that car, and with the right kind of action he could get the car and no one would ever be the wiser. Billy had come to hate this little town and it was time to get the hell out of White Settlement, Fort Worth, and maybe even Texas. That fancy old car had become a symbol for Billy – it was his ride to a new life, a better life. Watching the old man shuffle out of sight, "Badass" made up his mind – it was time to ratchet up the game another notch. The old fuck was going to have to die.

* * * * *

Three AM and it was still hot enough to fry an egg on the sidewalk. Billy moved among the shadows that covered the back of the old man's house. The guy was like so many of these old dumbasses: they either trusted the world too much or they couldn't afford the electricity because every light in and on the house was out. It was like the house was empty.

But the car had been sitting under the carport out front, under a tan canvas tarp. "Badass" had checked it before he gave himself the final "go-ahead" on his plan. This was going to be easy – go around to the back of the house; jimmy the door (it would probably be unlocked); slip inside; stick the old guy with the hunting knife he had stolen from a cousin years ago; find the keys; and drive off with the car. This was going to be the start of a whole new life.

Billy had been saving his money and he had pulled together $4,200 in cash from his various hidey-holes around the house. With the new car, his grubstake, and the open road ahead of him, Billy "Badass" Barnes was going to be free of "Liberator Village." No more crappy little house, no more penny-ante jobs, Billy was jetting for the big time! He had paid his dues and he figured that he could move from one hot spot to another and live the same life he had been excelling at for the last few years. He had put a timer on one of the lights in his den and turned off the mail for a month. Nobody ever came over; he wouldn't be missed for quite some time. Not until somebody came by to turn off the water or the electricity. From now on, though, he'd be living in apartments or hotels. The trick was to just keep moving and with this car there was no stopping him.

Billy slowly felt his way, moving towards the door he knew was about a third of the way down the back of house . . .there. No noise so far and, sure enough, the damn door was unlocked.

"It's like you're expecting me, old man," Billy thought to himself, "like you know someone's coming to put you out of your misery and you're making it easy for 'em."

"Well," Billy whispered as he slipped into the house and shut the door behind him, "here I am."

The first thing Billy noticed about the inside of the house was that it was even hotter inside than it was outside.

"The old fart must never use his air conditioning," thought Billy, "guess he can't afford it. Maybe the reason he hardly ever uses his car is 'cause he can't afford the gas."

As Billy moved deeper into the house, he started to sweat like a pig. His shirt was sticking to him all over after only a minute or so. The air felt weird, too, like something you'd expect in a jungle. It smelled like something out of a jungle, too. He was ready to find the old guy, slip the big knife into his guts a few times and get out of there. Get free. It was then that he stumbled into the refrigerator and the metal door was so hot that it actually burned him.

"DAMN!" Billy hissed between clinched teeth. His arm, where it had made contact with the fridge was hurting like hell and he was scared that he had made enough noise to rouse the dead and maybe even the old fucker living here. The place was really hot and wet and misty, Billy imagined this must be what a steam bath felt like . . . a steam bath in Hell!

What was happening to him . . . his eyes were teary and he was having trouble keeping them open against the sweat running down his forehead . . . his legs were trembling and his back felt funny, it hurt and it tingled and it burned all at the same time. This was fuckin' weird!

"I'm glad you're finally here, Billy, you have no idea how much I've come to hate this place; I will be so happy to be gone from it."

Billy heard the voice more in his head than he did through his ears. It sounded all calm and uppity, kind of like that last teacher at community college, the one that had told Billy, "I know you can make it; all you have to do is apply yourself," all the time the both of them knowing it was never going to happen . . .

"I can't say much for your little planet here but it does seem to be abundantly populated with creatures like yourself. Full of life, full of mischief, but you make excellent slaves once you've been broken and you are so adaptable to so many different worlds with the right kind of . . . modifications. But the best part is that no one will ever miss you, the life you lived made sure of that. Actually, the herd will be overjoyed that you're gone."

Billy tried to bring the knife up and slash at where he thought the voice was coming from but he couldn't *feel* his body anymore. He couldn't see anything anymore, either, but he sensed currents in the air, or whatever he was surrounded with, move as something big and slimy moved next to him, seemed to push him in the direction of what he vaguely remembered as being the front of the . . house?

"But you're my last, my *shenzi* friend, I can get off this uncivilized lump of molten copper you call a planet and be free to get back to a real world! You complete my contract, Billy! I needed only one more slave to fill my ship and YOU are it! Don't you feel good about finally doing something with your life?"

Billy heard what he thought must be laughter as his captor/tormentor/host shivered against him. He wanted so badly to strike out at the thing, to stab it or punch it; anything to drive the damn thing away from him and maybe, just maybe get out of this place alive.

Everything began to move like liquid now. Billy couldn't feel anything anymore, couldn't see anything, either. He sure as hell smelled whatever it was in there with him but he was getting more and more confused as he breathed in the shit that filled the house. It was like what people said about drowning, he thought, and he could feel the panic rising from deep in the middle of him, rising to the surface like a big wood roach drawling up his spine, headed for his mouth. He couldn't even tell if he was real any more or not, if he had turned into some kind of gas or he had melted or what. All he knew was that something horrible was happening to him and it was all happening way too fast. He opened his mouth to scream . . . and that old roach crawled right in.

"Go ahead and try to scream, Billy," . . . the voice came again, distracted this time, like the thing was too busy doing something (flying its space ship?) to bother with him. Billy was suddenly a kid again, and his dad was up in the front seat of their old car, not even glancing back, just flipping back a response to shut the kid up . . . "go ahead and scream because no one will be able to hear you for awhile."

And Billy did scream now. He screamed loud and hard and for as long as he could. Billy Barnes screamed for all he was worth because he figured, if he didn't make anyone hear him now, nothing human would ever hear him scream again.

Golden

I stood inside a rainbow
A mist of flaming vapor
Kissed by sun and cloud
Descending all around me

Some say that cannot happen
One must be far away to see
But I know
At magic moments
Like noon
In the mist
In the mountains
Rainbows fall straight
To the ground

I stood there
In that sacred place
With fire falling all around
And for one shining moment
I was golden

Wendy Easterling
©2009

The Tomb of Ilaria
By Sharon Robb-Chism
©2009

Delan, on his first unlucky visit, was presented at court dragged between two guards, their bent elbows under his armpits. With bleeding knuckles, his hands were tied at his crossed wrists, and his legs bound just below his knees. His escorts propped him to his feet, then stood silently at his side. Delan waited, the dozens of hanging lamps and scented candles in the throne room putting peacock highlights in his raven hair--which fell in disarray, due to recent exertion, to just below his shoulders. A split lower lip, and blood still oozing from his slightly hawked nose, gave color to an otherwise pale complexion. One eye was slowly swelling shut and would no doubt soon be the color of a damask plum. His good eye, the clear, cold blue of a winter sky, regarded his Queen with a spark of humor.

"Your present condition, Swordsman, contradicts your reputation," the Queen said. Around her clustered a dozen ministers, two priests, three ladies in waiting, her Court Physic, and a dwarf dressed in motley and bells, all looking at Delan as if the room had suddenly filled with a nauseating smell.

He gave her a lopsided grin. "You have not seen the present condition of the other three guards you sent to escort me."

"I was also told you had a difficulty with authority, but could be charming. I find you insolent." She waved a pale hand at the two guards. "Unbind him."

93

While his surviving captors turned to undo their work of only a half hour before, Delan took an appraising look at Oresti, Queen of all Ruala.

Her hair was the color of antique gold, elaborately dressed and circled in gemmed filigree. Her lips were sensual, but pale, her eyes tawny brown with a gaze as direct as a shaft of sunlight through a latticed window. The skin of face, neck, shoulders and décolletage was smooth and unmarked, but its milky whiteness was marred by an unhealthy tint of blue. Once freed, Delan clenched and unclenched his hands a few times, then, of habit, reached to his left hip to reassure himself of his sword, which he could not, as he recollected it had been confiscated.

Queen Oresti rose from the ornate carved chair of state made for her grandfather, who had usurped the throne from his brother and claimed Ruala for himself. There were rumors Oresti's sister, Kesha, hoped to repeat history.

Oresti stepped from the dais and approached him. Behind her the many attendants hovered like drones, but she waved them away, and they retreated to a respectful distance. She was tall, and her lioness gaze was nearly on a level with his own, presently monocular one.

"As you observe from my unique coloring," she said, "I am a dying woman."

"Alas, it is the fate all living creatures must reconcile themsleves with."

Her royal brow furrowed. "Do not bore me with philosophy or religious dogma. My impending demise is not the design of nature, but the design of my enemies. I have been poisoned."

"It grieves me to hear it, but as I am neither a powerful sorcerer, a learned physic, nor a devout priest, I fail to see how I can be of service to you."

She gave him a smile even Delan, so well acquainted with the smiles of the fairer sex, could not read. "I have an errand I wish to send you on."

"Errand?" Delan was instantly more wary than his relaxed stance would convey. Errands for royalty often involved complications. "What errand could it be that one of your many minions could not perform just as easily?"

"My Court Physic, Ianis, informs me the poison now coursing through my body is extremely rare. The only thing rarer is its antidote. I want you to fetch me that antidote."

"You will forgive my ignorance, but how is it that you yet live if you have been poisoned?"

"That is the beauty, if you would call it that, of its actions. You see, this poison does not kill by convulsions, or asphyxia. No, it is much more insidious than that. It slowly weakens the body until its victim no longer has the strength to even swallow. Thus, in the end, you die of starvation. I am told I have a month, maybe less."

"And does your Highness know where this antidote may be found?"

The smile she gave him then was cold. "Oh yes. You will find it in the city of Brescia."

Delan willed himself not to blink. Brescia, the most accursed city in all of Ruala. A city so damned, so evil, due to the machinations of its ruling family, that even three hundred years after its last occupant ceased to breathe, few dared enter it. This despite the legend that the abandoned palace was filled with so much wealth a man, nor seven of his following generations, would be able to spend it all. Those who braved the ruins had either never returned, or come back stripped of their sanity.

"Surely, Highness, you do not think a trinket from Brescia will reverse the poison?"

"No, I desire neither gem, nor gold, nor magic talisman. The only medicine that will save me is the powdered bone of Ilaria."

This time Delan did blink. The Lady Ilaria was the last member of the rulers of Brescia. Like a spider sucking the fluids from a fly, she had drained the land and people around her until there was nothing left for her to feed on. As her city fell into chaos, so did Ilaria's mind, until her few remaining servants poisoned her, and lay her body in a tomb purported to be lined with gold.

Delan, his voice remaining calm, said, "Ah, a poison to counteract a poison."

"Just so."

"And if I succeed in this errand?"

"Bring me as little as one finger bone from her tomb, and you will leave my city with enough jewels and gold to build your own palace."

"And if I refuse or fail?"

She stepped closer, a feral glitter in her tawny eyes. "If I die, Swordsman, you die. Then we shall both discover if the priests have lied to us all these years about the joys of paradise."

*   *   *   *   *

His sword returned to him, Delan left the city and traveled through the desert for three days. By the second day he knew he was being followed. He had expected no less. Whoever had poisoned the Queen would not wish her restored to health.

Late afternoon on the fourth day he arrived at the oasis shrine of Cimra. Under the shade of a palm grove, the turrets and gilded dome of a small temple welcomed pilgrims pausing to refresh themselves. In front of the temple, its natural waterline confined and reconfigured into a large rectangle within a low wall, its top set with colored tiles, was the oasis pool. At intervals along the wall were scrolled iron stands, from which hung long-handled ladles, so cupped human hands would not sully the pure water.

To one side of the temple stood the residence of the priest. Behind this was a garrison which housed a dozen guards, their job to make sure the pool was not fouled, a crime for which the punishment was death.

As Delan entered the grove, he noted many other travelers taking their ease. To the west were scattered a half-dozen tents of the horse tribesmen, their hobbled mounts grazing among them. To the east, a small caravan of seven or eight mules, still burdened with their heavy packs, drank from a long stone trough. In front of a large black tent three caravaneers sat cross-legged, cursing and tossing dice.

Delan dismounted and led his horse to another trough, then went to the pool, dipped a wooden ladle into its clear water, and drank. Much refreshed, he went about putting up his small traveler's tent in the shade of a juvenile palm. As the sky went from pale turquoise to deep lapis, and the sun blazed a final goodbye to the day, Delan sat relaxed, eating a sparse meal of dried apricots, unleavened bread, and cured goat's meat. Around him, as torches bloomed in the inky darkness, the rasping sound of cicadas replaced the murmurs of men and the occasional braying of mules. With three more days of desert travel ahead of him, Delan entered his tent, lay down on his blankets and gave every appearance of being asleep.

96

Even the cicadas had ceased their noise when, above his head, came the sound of renting fabric followed by the gleam of a sword. In the quickness of a heartbeat, Delan rolled to the opposite side of his tent, so the sword impaled only his blankets. With equal speed, he exited through the back. His assailant had unwisely waited for him at the front, and thus was startled to feel the point of Delan's sword pricking the nape of his neck.

"Who sent you?" Delan demanded.

He received no answer. Instead, his assailant whirled around and the loud clash of steel meeting steel rang through the palms. Delan blocked an expert thrust aimed at his throat. After four more clashes, which sent the mules to braying again, Delan had maneuvered the stranger to the other side of the tent. As a fierce blow arched toward his neck, he gracefully ducked. His opponent's sword bit deep into the juvenile palm--and stuck.

Delan heard a muffled oath, but by then the razored tip of his sword was at the assailant's throat just below the dark wrap of cloth that concealed the lower half of the person's face. The turns of cloth also covered his head, so only the eyes were visible. Yet, even in the dim light of the risen half-moon, there was no mistaking the rage that possessed their owner.

"Who sent you?" Delan demanded again. From the direction of the barracks he could hear the jingling of chain mail and the rattle of grieves, as the night guard rushed to investigate the cause of the disturbance.

In moments three soldiers came to a noisy halt, their swords drawn. One of them held up a lantern. "What business goes on here?"

"For some reason, this man tried to kill me," Delan said, his sword still poised a hairs-width away from the pulse-point in the man's neck.

The first guard peered at the supposed assailant and said, 'Who are you? Speak up!"

Silence.

The second guard growled, "We have ways of making you talk. Do not force us to use them."

Delan, keeping his blade in place, said, "Let's see who you are." And with a deft movement, unwound the cloth concealing the man's identity. The face revealed was that of a sloe-eyed woman, framed by a newly loosed tumble of auburn hair.

The lantern holder stepped closer. "Ha, a harlot." Then gave Delan a wink.

Delan smiled. "I think not." He had observed, between her lowered brows, the red-inked tattoo of a wavy-armed star of eight points. "I believe she is of the Hune, the Queen's elite guard."

The first soldier gave a derisive laugh. "Pah, there are no women among the Hune." The woman turned her fierce gaze on him and spit in his face. "And what would a sniveling water-guard know of the Hune?"

"Why you..." the soldier raised his own sword, as did the first.

Delan held up his hand. "Hold. To kill one of the Hune is treason. Harm her, and you will find yourselves taken out into the desert, dribbled with sweet syrups, and staked over a fire-ant hill."

The two guards lowered their swords and took a step back. The woman sneered.

"You may go on about your night's duties. I will find what has sent a member of so elite a fighting group out to kill me."

The three guards hesitated, then, apparently deciding Delan could handle the situation himself, and having no wish to involve themselves with the Hune, departed.

Delan eyed the woman a moment and admired the challenging lift of her chin, as if she dared him to slice the pale throat beneath it. "You were not sent by the Queen."

"No. I came of my own will."

"Who are you, and why are you attempting to kill me?"

"I am Makara," she said with obvious pride. "I came to reclaim the honor of the Hune." Delan lowered his sword, then with a jerk, freed the other weapon from the palm and returned it to her. 'How have I dishonored the Hune?"

She snorted, then sheathed the sword. "You could not dishonor the Hune, but the Queen has by giving you this task instead of one of her own. She bribes you with riches, when the Hune would have performed this errand out of loyalty only."

Delan's perfect dark brows rose a fraction. "And do you know what my errand is?"

"You are to bring the medicine that will cure the Queen's illness."

"And, you are also aware of where this medicine is located?"

Delan let his eyes, both fully open, appraise her. In the semi-dark he could see very little, considering she was dressed in men's clothes, other than she was of medium height, obviously skilled with a weapon, and was still poised to kill him should he give her the chance.

"In...In Brescia," she said.

"You do not fear to go there?"

Before she could reply, three men dressed in the garb of horse tribesmen emerged from the darkness, swords raised. As one, Delan and Makara faced the strangers, weapons at the ready. Delan neatly severed the first man's wrist. The man howled as his hand, still gripping his sword, dropped into the sparse grass. Makara, with the lightning reflexes of years of training among the Hune, dodged the sword thrust of another man aimed at her chest, and with a vicious scream, decapitated him. The third assassin ran toward the temple. Delan reached into his boot and flung the knife secreted there. The assassin fell across the low, tiled wall, the blood seeping from his neck polluting the purity of the oasis pool. Some distance off could be heard the weakening cries of the maimed man.

Delan strode to the pool and quickly pulled the dead man from the water before anyone could see the desecration. He retrieved his knife from the man's neck and returned it to his boot, then turned to Makara, who had followed him. "Do you recognize him?"

"No, but these alley dogs are not horse tribesmen, no matter how they are dressed. Had they been, we would have died in silence with arrows in our hearts."

Delan nodded. "I suspect they were sent to make sure my errand did not succeed."

At that moment, the three guards who had investigated the previous disturbance returned with four more of their number. The first exclaimed, "You two, again?" Then looked at the dead man laying at their feet. "And who is this? You have killed a tribesman. Why?"

Delan stood at graceful ease. "He is not a tribesman. Nor is his fellow, who you will find over there," he gestured toward his tent, "whose head, alas, has been parted from his body. You may also find a third, missing his right hand. At the rate he was bleeding I doubt he got far."

Makara remained silent, her lowered sword dripping crimson.

A rustle of armor as the soldiers parted heralded the arrival of the priest. It was very apparent he was angered at being wakened at such a late--or more closely early--hour. "Who are you to interrupt the sacred peace of this oasis? It is well known throughout Ruala the places of water are sanctuary. Explain this breech of Rualan law." As he spoke, the many braids of the priest's beard quivered and danced.

Delan shrugged. "If I knew who they were, I would tell you. As I don't, I cannot."

The priest cast his black-eyed gaze on Makara. "And you, woman, what do you here?"

Makara returned the man's stare with green-eyed coldness. "I am of the Hune. I do not explain myself to priests, or anyone."

The soldiers mumbled. The word assassin was heard. Makara's gaze raked over them with contempt. "The Hune are not assassins. But observe closely the fate of those who are." She pointed her still dripping sword at the dead man.

Around the grisly tableau a group of people had gathered, some bearing torches. Delan noticed the three caravaneers, along with two dozen angered horse tribesmen, who obviously thought one of their own had been slain.

Delan spoke to the priest, "We meant no offense to the laws of sanctuary. This man and his two fellows, who are not tribesmen," he emphasized again, "attacked us. We merely defended ourselves."

The priest, noticing the tension among the onlookers, as did Delan, said, "It appears you attract persons of unwholesome character. Depart, Swordsman, and take this she-devil with you, for even the Hune are not exempt from the sanctuary laws. If you are still here at daybreak, I will instruct the guards to seize you and your goods. The cells in the temple catacomb are very unpleasant, do not risk a visit."

"I do not listen to—"

Delan cut Makara off. "I will, of course, do as you request."

*   *   *   *   *

The priest had allowed them to refill their water skins and flasks, and by the time the sun rose above the gathering heat-haze they were five miles from Cimra. The landscape thus illuminated was comprised of rolling hills of reddish, barren rock and sun-baked earth. As the day wore on, a light yet desiccating wind began to blow.

100

Delan, his face wrapped much as Makara's had been and was again, squinted into the distance, hoping the wind would not get stronger, and wondering where he might take shelter if it did. Makara rode uninvited, but not unobserved, some distance behind him. They had not spoken since leaving the oasis. As Delan rounded the next hill in his path, the wind swept from its crest and gusted over his head. He halted his horse in the meager shade, then pulled the cloth away from his face.

Eventually, Makara rode up beside him and did the same. She turned her leaf-green gaze to him and asked, "Have you ever seen Brescia?"

Delan took a sip from his water flask, wiped his lips, then said, "Yes. In my travels I have come near to it. However, I have had no occasion to enter."

She smiled. "The possibility of treasure did not entice you?"

"If I want treasure, there are easier places to acquire it than Brescia."

She wiped beads of sweat from her forehead. The red tattoo of the Hune stood out like a burn. "What is the medicine you must bring back?"

"So, you don't know the whole story. How will you honor the Hune if, not knowing what I am sent for, you kill me?"

She shrugged. "With your death, the Queen will instruct one of us how to find this cure."

"Let me instruct you instead. I am sent to bring back one of the bones from Ilaria's tomb. Ground into powder, it is the only thing that will cure the Queen of a rare poison. Do you still wish to follow me?"

Though her face paled, she answered, "The Hune are not cowards."

"Against the known. What of the unknown? Have you tested your courage against ghosts and demons? Could you face the shade of Ilaria herself, and not run screaming into the desert?"

Makara's chin rose a fraction. "Could you?"

Delan laughed. "I suppose I'll find out."

They traveled long into the night, to take advantage of the cooler air. Around midnight they set up their tents in the lee of a shallow wash, and made a meager fire from dead thorn branches. Overhead, brittle, cold stars shimmered in a sky dark as mourning velvet, while a waxing moon the color of antique ivory slowly climbed across the heavens.

Makara, picking at a piece of bread, looked at Delan. "Why do you persist in this errand? You could have left the city and disappeared."

Delan, having accepted the challenge for reasons of his own, did not feel like sharing them. He shrugged. "I have a curious nature. Brescia is a curious place."

"It is a place of madness."

"It is a ruin."

She snorted. "As you say, a ruin. But a cursed ruin. Do you believe in demons?"

Delan popped a dried apricot in his mouth, then smiled at her. "Oh yes. Don't you?"

She shivered, but did not answer.

Far out in the desert a hyena gave a yipping laugh and was answered by its pack-mates. From very close a pebble crunched. Delan was on his feet, sword drawn. Makara instinctively covered his back. They stood, shoulder blades almost touching, as two figures, again dressed as horse tribesmen, emerged from the darkness. One gestured toward the crackling fire. "How kind of you to light a beacon to guide us."

Delan said, "It was the only way to draw you out. You see how successful it has been."

The second man, apparently thinking the woman the easier target, lunged at Makara. She sidestepped and put a neat slice in his calf. Before she could turn, the first man swung at her. She ducked the blow aimed at her neck, but caught the tip of the man's sword on her upper arm. Delan dispatched the man bleeding from his calf, then yanked the second man away from Makara. She made to finish him, but Delan said quickly, "No! I'd like to confirm who sent him." Unwisely, the man spit in Delan's face. Delan slipped his boot knife from its hiding place and jabbed it into the meaty part of the man's thigh. To his credit, the assassin only sucked in a deep breath.

"Who sent you?" Delan purred.

"Speak, dog of Kestis. You have nothing to lose, as we will kill you in either case." Makara's sword point hovered within inches of the terrified man's left eye.

"And may Kestis the Unholy curse me before I tell you," the man spat back.

Delan said, "It doesn't matter. I already know who sent you. It was the Queen's Physic."

The man's eyes widened, verifying.

Makara said, "Master Ianis?"

"Of course."

She looked annoyed. "Why would Master Ianis want to poison the Queen?"

"He is a close, but secret, confidant of the Queen's sister, Kesha. She who is so eager to take Orestis place on their grandfather's throne. Is it not true, our good friend?" Delan wiggled the knife in the man's leg.

This time he did howl, and was answered by one of the far off hyenas. His lips tight across his pond-green teeth, he sputtered, "Yes. It's true."

Delan looked at Makara. "You see, all he needed was a bit of encouragement."

"Ianis," Makara snarled. "I'll kill that traitorous swine."

"You needn't bother, the Queen has plans for him."

The poor, impaled man apparently decided to cut his losses, turned and made to run. Delan caught him. "Please, before you go, I would like my knife back." He reached down and jerked the weapon from the man's leg. Another howl.

"You're not going to let him go!" Makara, her sword still aimed at the hapless would-be assassin, glared at Delan.

"I see no harm in it. Of course, we will have to take his horse and water, but other than that, he is free."

Makara smiled. "Yes, let the desert take him."

The man ran, injured leg or no.

Delan looked at Makara, who was examining the slash in her left arm. "How bad is it?"

"Not to the bone, but deep."

He pulled back her bloody shirt sleeve and inspected the gaping wound. "I'll have to seal it with fire."

She nodded.

He put his knife blade into the glowing coals of the fire. Moments later, Delan lay the blade into the wound. There was a hissing, and a smell of seared flesh.

Makara made not a sound.

*   *   *   *   *

At dawn of the third day, Delan and Makara paused on a rocky promontory and looked out over a vast, flat plain. The molten ball of the sun blushed the sky a deep rose and mauve shadows stretched away from the ruins thus revealed, as if trying to escape. Brescia spread across the center of the plain like mold on cheese--a city of crumbling stone, fallen towers and abandoned houses. At Brescia's navel rose the crenelated walls and spearlike minarets of the palace.

The sun rose higher. Heat waves distorted the landscape. The sky lost its healthy blush and became once again a sheet of bleached-out blue. In neither sky nor land, did anything alive move.

Delan said, "Now is a good time to promise you won't, once we're in the city, try and kill me."

"I make you no such promise."

He turned cold blue eyes to her, "You don't know what's in there. It may be more dangerous than I am."

"Then, once I have the Queen's cure, I'll kill you both."

Delan gave her a teasing laugh, then urged his horse down the narrow path that led to the plain. Behind him, he could hear Makara cursing.

It took them half the day to reach the city. The closer they got, the heavier the air became, the heat more intense. Eyes narrowed to mere slits, they watched the city loom larger and larger, until they reached the first buildings--low huts, strewn like mud-wasp nests around the wall that circled the city, and baked hard as flint.

The main gate into Brescia was two stories tall, set with iron, and branded with the sign of the family who had ruled for five centuries. The gate opened inward, one half lying on its side, while the other half clung to the wall by one enormous rusted hinge.

Delan rode under a high stone arch, its wide shadow giving a moment's relief from the sun. The silence was a heavy weight. The crunch of the horses' hooves on the baked street

104

echoed off the pitted walls of the buildings that leaned in over them. They passed long-abandoned shops, small chapels, and private houses. Dried and cracked fountains dribbled dust. Broken indigo tiles lay in the dirt like chips of fallen sky.

And the smell. A pervading presence, noisome and vile, that seeped from the pores of Brescia like the perfume of a carnivorous plant.

The horses balked.

Delan dismounted. "Hobble them. And take your water flask. I do not trust the wells here."

Swords drawn, they walked on, neck-cloths pulled back over their faces. The dirt street changed to one of worn cobbles. The buildings showed traces of painted murals, pitted and scoured by blown sand. Deep in the crevices of ornate stone molding winked bits of gold leaf. They traversed a courtyard, discovering a large iron birdcage. On close inspection they realized its last occupant had not been dove or finch, but a child.

Makara backed away from the cage. "Where is this tomb we must find?"

"Somewhere near the palace."

"How do you know?"

Without answering, Delan walked on. He cut through a narrow alley, stepping over the bleached bones of a dead mule, its owner lying next to it. They passed small orchards of withered trees, tiled reflecting pools, their aquatic mirrors evaporated, broken urns housing skeletal palms, and always the dead blank eyes of glassless windows--watching.

Delan led Makara down two more streets, through another alley, then across a large plaza, where stood a huge stone figure of a winged lion, paused on its haunches, paw raised to strike--or would have been, had the paw not been broken near the elbow. Littered around the courtyard were more scattered, weathered bones. Beyond the courtyard was another wall, and another fallen gate. Beyond the gate rose the palace.

Makara glared at Delan, her eyes the only green, living thing in the city. "You've been here before."

"Yes." Delan approached the gate.

"That's why the Queen sent you for the antidote, rather than one of the Hune."

"Yes."

"You've seen the tomb."

"Yes, although at the time, I had no reason to open it." He walked past the fallen gate.

"Does Master Ianis know you've been here?"

Delan said, "No. I suspect he is praying fervently that I don't return."

"Why didn't you tell me all this?"

He pulled his neck-cloth away and grinned at her. "You might have thought me mad."

Across the plaza, and next to the entrance to the palace, stood a small temple. Delan pointed to it. "The tomb is in there."

And it was. The sarcophagus of carved and gilded marble sat on a plinth of three stone steps. There was no effigy of the dead Ilaria on its lid.

Delan ascended the steps.

Makara, pulling her own neck-cloth away from her face, followed him. "What now?"

"We open it."

Together, with a scraping noise that echoed off the walls, they pushed the great lid aside and looked in. Legend was proved true. The inside of the sarcophagus glowed with the mellow, buttery light of gold. Ilaria, however, was not present. The tomb was empty.

"Dogs of Kestis, now what do we do?" Makara said.

"We look elsewhere."

Delan had been almost sure the tomb would be empty. It did not mean Ilaria no longer resided in her city. The rumors of gold and gems buried with her would have been too great a temptation to grave robbers, who, due to their line of work, tended to be less superstitious than most. The attendants who poisoned her would have hidden the body in a less obvious place. The ostentatious sarcophagus was a diversion.

But those long ago attendants, wishing to save the remnants of the city from her madness, did not foresee that soon after Ilaria died, drawn by the cruelty and bloodlust, something else would visit her city, and stay. Something that needed neither gold nor gems to survive, but used them as bait.

Makara stepped away from the sarcophagus. "The palace?"

"I'm afraid so. I would try the throne room."

When they opened the verdigris bronze doors of the palace, the smell hit them like a blast of air from the underworld. Makara gagged. "Everything in Brescia is dust, what's causing the stench?"

"I have a guess." Delan, not unaffected by the carrion odor, breathed shallowly.

Little was left of the splendor of Ilaria's palace. Lush draperies, fine paintings, rare carpets and carved furniture were all gone. Covering the floor were small tesserae set in a pattern of swirling water, most of the gilded pieces missing, leaving gaps like pulled teeth. From the walls hung great bronze oil lamps, their gems picked off. The ceiling of the throne room soared three stories over their heads, its gilding and frescos protected by the height.
The throne itself was intact. Carved, jeweled and draped with cloth, it glowed in a shaft of sunlight streaming through a high window.

Makara froze.

Delan let out a slow breath.

Seated upon the throne was a woman. She appeared to be asleep. Her skin was smooth and pale as cream, her hair, bright as burnished copper, was dressed with pearls. A robe of deep wine velvet covered her shoulders. Under it she wore a gown of green silk embroidered in silver. Her small hands rested lightly on the arms of the great chair, and her bare feet, their dainty nails painted crimson, rested on a brocade footstool.

Makara whispered, "Ilaria?"

The sleeping woman opened her eyes. They were the color of bright blood. She smiled, and her rosy lips framed teeth black and jagged as obsidian chips. "Welcome to Brescia." The voice was harsh and deep.

Makara stepped back, her eyes wide. "Delan, what is that?"
Delan answered, "A demon, of course."

The thing that had been Ilaria rose from the throne. The smell of corruption lapped at their senses like waves on a beach.

"Kill it!" Makara shouted.

The demon-Ilaria laughed, a guttural sound a dying animal might make. "Yes, kill me."

108

Delan, his sword poised, said, "It's already dead."

Retching, Makara backed another step. "Then let's get out of here."

"Fly, fly, little fledglings," the demon said, descending the last step of the dais. She who was not Ilaria waved a pale hand, "Fly to where it is safe." Then laughed again.

Delan stood his ground. Makara, recovering her nerve, stood next to him. He said with calm, "You can't outrun it. It's a game, like a cat with a mouse."

"Well, I am no mouse." Makara raised her sword.

The demon continued to laugh. "Go ahead, warrior, pierce me. Do your best. Here, I will make it easy for you." It held out a graceful arm, the wrist circled in a gold bracelet of tiny charms.

Before Delan could stop her, Makara swung her sword, then watched with horror as it swept through the thing's arm as if through smoke.

Delan pulled Makara's sword-arm down. "I told you, you can't kill it. It's already dead. It's using Ilaria's body as a shell...as camouflage."

The demon-Ilaria smiled her obsidian smile at Delan, then gave her body a lewd caress. "A rather nice shell, don't you think, Swordsman? Want a taste?"

"Alas, no."

It came closer, its bloody gaze regarding him with hatred. "Why not?"

"I fear, like a mantis, you would eat your lover."

"Delan!" Makara cried, backing away.

The thing grabbed Makara's arm. "Then maybe I'll make a sweetmeat of this one." Makara screamed, struggling against the deceiving strength in the feminine fingers that gripped her like talons.

Delan said, "Maybe not."

The demon-Ilaria, drooling in anticipation of a fresh meal, pulled Makara closer, snuffling over her like a dog. With its leathery tongue, it licked around Makara's neck and ear, then looked at Delan. "And who's to stop me, Swordsman, you?"

"Delan, I have no wish to be this thing's lunch. For Kestis' sake, do something." Red welts were already forming where the demon's tongue had touched Makara's flesh.

"Do something, do something," the demon mocked, it's voice that of a screeching bird.

Delan backed away, circling toward the dais.

"Coward!" Makara shouted.

Delan kept circling.

Dragging Makara, the demon-Ilaria turned with him, its blood-red gaze darkened to garnet.

When Delan reached the dais, he backed up two steps, then quickly unhooked the water flask from his belt. Dropping his sword, he pulled the stopper from the flask and flung its contents over the demon's head.

Like water tossed into hot coals, it hissed and spat, creating a cloud of acrid smoke. The demon shrieked.

Leaping from the dais, Delan yelled at Makara, "Your water flask. Quick!"

Makara, free of her tormentor, fumbled at her belt, then tossed it to him. He threw it at the floor in the demon's path. The pottery shattered and water from the sacred oasis pool splashed over the thing's dainty feet, causing them to shrivel and blacken. More smoke clogged their noses and burned their eyes. The shrill screaming pierced their ears like knives.

That which had been Ilaria retreated to the throne. In her retreat, the fine robe became dust, the silk gown cobweb, as the three-century-old body of the beautiful, but mad, Ilaria writhed and decayed. Slowly the shrieks became moans, the moans a whimper--then a heavy silence.

The noxious vapors rose to the ceiling. What was left of Lady Ilaria was what they should have discovered in her tomb--a dried jumble of bone.

The two stood silent for a moment, then Delan said, "Still want to kill me?"

"Unfortunately, I cannot. You have saved my life. The code of the Hune demands that I spare you."

"Are you sorry?"

Makara gave him a wry smile. "No."

"Good, we will have a much more pleasant ride home." Delan stepped toward the dais, knelt, and picked something from the floor.

"What is it?" Makara asked, rubbing her arm where the demon had gripped it.

Delan held out his hand. In his sword-callused palm was a finger bone.

*   *   *   *   *

On their ride back to the oasis shrine of Cimra, they came across the body of the assailant Delan had freed. From the condition of the remains, it appeared the hyenas had spared him a more lingering death.

The priest of the oasis temple, not happy to see them, was mollified by the gift of a large ruby set in gold. For it had been the demon who had stripped Brescia of its treasure, which Delan and Makara found while exploring the palace. They had left it, thinking they could find no safer hiding place. They also discovered another source of the smell--an oubliette filled with the rotting corpses of those who had previously challenged the demon--a larder of sorts, from which it feasted when nothing fresh presented itself.

"You may stay the night," the priest offered, holding the ruby to the sun, "But do not disrupt our peace."

*   *   *   *   *

Three days later they were back in the throne room of Queen Oresti.

"Have you brought my cure?" Her voice was weak, her coloring gray.

"Yes, Highness," Delan gave his Queen a knowing look, "But, I would have a word before you take it."

Her attendants whispered. Her ladies in waiting twittered. Her Physic protested, "You have little time, my Queen, take this cure that will save you without delay."

Makara glared. "Your concern is false, Ianis. If your hired assassins had succeeded, we would have no cure."

The court gasped.

"That's a lie! Besides, how do we know he has brought back a bone from Ilaria's tomb? It could be something dug from a common grave." The Physic gave Delan his most officious look, but his body trembled.

The Queen raised her hand, the rings glinting in the light of the oil lamps. "You accuse my Physic of some crime?"

"Not yet," Delan said. "However, before you take this cure, I would ask you to test it on he who recommended it to you. He who is so knowledgeable in the ways of poisons and their antidotes, and is such a good friend to Lady Kesha, your sister."

Queen Oresti motioned her Physic to come forward. "You thought me a fool, didn't you, Ianis? I knew you had poisoned me. Fortunately, I also knew of someone who could retrieve that which you thought impossible to secure."

"Don't believe this barbarian," Master Ianis said, beads of perspiration glistening on his forehead, "Take the cure, my Queen, before...before it is too late."

"That sounds very much like a threat." The Queen's lioness gaze caused her Physic to shrink back.

The royal dwarf grinned.

Delan proffered a small leather pouch which contained the finger bone. "It is from Ilaria, I promise you."

Makara said, "I vouch for this Swordsman, Highness. I was with him when he took the bone."

A mortar and pestle were brought forward, along with a flask of wine. The bone was crushed into a fine powder. A goblet was filled with the wine and a pinch of bone powder sprinkled into it. The goblet was offered to the Physic. With a nervous glance at his Queen, he reached out a suddenly palsied hand and took it. "It is a waste of —"

"Drink!" the Queen snapped. "Or I'll have Makara of the Hune force it down your throat. After you enjoy a few swallows, I'll send the dregs to my loving, traitorous sister."

The court became silent as the streets of Brescia. The Physic, his eyes wild with fear, hesitated, then put the goblet to his lips and drank. The court waited. The Queen waited.

Seconds went by. Master Ianis smiled, apparently in the belief the bone was too old to be effective. Alas, his own knowledge should had warned him not to be premature. In the next second his face blanched, his eyes bulged, and small strangling noises escaped between whitened stretched lips. The goblet dropped to the floor with a clang. The Queen's Physic followed it with a thud, as his head hit the marble.

The court took in a collective breath. Two of the ladies in waiting began to cry. The royal dwarf, in pantomime of some shaman, shook his staff of bells over the dead man.

The Queen looked at Delan, who said, "Poison to counteract a poison is still...poison."

"And what of me? Will this powder work?"

"Drink, Highness, with no fear. I do not think Ianis lied. That which poisons you now will, as he promised, be counteracted by that which poisoned Ilaria and remains in her bones."

The royal dwarf picked up the goblet and handed it to his Queen. It was refilled with wine, and a large pinch of bone added. Queen Orestis paused a moment, then drank it all.

Once again the court was quiet. Seconds passed. Then minutes. The Queen showed no signs of eminent demise. She looked at Delan. "If by this time tomorrow I am still alive, I will consider your errand completed and reward you as I promised. In the meantime, you are my...guest."

The next day the Queen was not merely still alive, but much restored. Her color less gray, her appetite renewed. Delan was granted his reward, which he requested the Queen to hold in safe keeping, as his lifestyle was not conducive to carrying large quantities of treasure around Ruala.

Before leaving Queen Oresti's city, Delan met with Makara in a small tavern just inside the main gate. They sat outside, under a latticed shade, enjoying the finest wine the merchant carried.

Makara, her green eyes sparkling, said, "So, the jewels of Brescia had enticed you after all."

"Yes. Years ago I did think of searching for the treasure."

"How did the Queen come to hear of you?"

He gave her an enigmatic smile. "The Queen and I have had dealings before. When she suspected Master Ianis, she...sent for me. The scuffle with her guards was to keep Ianis from knowing we were in collusion. We also didn't want Kesha any the wiser. Master Ianis probably wasn't too worried his hired thugs failed to kill me, since no one has ever returned from Brescia alive or sane. Our miraculous return to court was his death-knell."

"Did you know Ilaria's tomb would be empty?"

"I suspected it." Delan began to peel an orange.

"And, did you know there was a demon lurking in the palace?"

"Yes."

She glared. "Yet, you let me walk into that place with no warning? Had you seen that...that thing before?"

"No, only smelled it. You must agree, it's a very distinctive smell."

"How did you know the sacred water would kill it?"

"I didn't. But I had a hunch that the sacred and the profane woudn't mix." He grinned.

"Just how did you plan for us to escape if it hadn't worked?"

He shrugged. "I have a curious nature. I would have found something."

She took a sip of her wine. On her neck and cheek the welts from the demon's tongue were nearly gone. "Your curious nature almost got us eaten, or thrown into that disgusting pit."

"True, but now we both know, if we see a demon again, we won't go screaming into the desert. Are you sorry we left the treasure?"

She shook her head. "No, the Hune have no need of such things."

"Are you sure?" He held out his hand. In his palm rested a section of fruit. "Orange?"

Next to the piece of fruit was a large sapphire and diamond ring, a small souvenir of the treasures of Brescia.

Makara smiled and took the ring and the fruit. "Thank you."

Much later, in silvery moonlight, Delan left the capital of Ruala with nothing but his horse and his sword.

The Sorcerer's Headphones
By Stephen Sanders
©1977

"It's 2:32 in the morning and just north of 36 degrees here at KROW radio in Wattle, Texas. Top of the morning to you from 'cockle-doodle-do' radio! Now, here's the new one from Cody Snow, with Jessi Manley and the Skyboys coming up!"

Joel Fox, disc jockey, looked up at the large white-faced clock on the wall. The station had recently let two of the newer jockeys go and everyone else was pulling nine-hour shifts. Switching off the mike, Joel brought up the feed from a CD player. The CD going out over the air was one of the special mixes that Joel made up to give him some time away from the mike. This one included seven songs, ten commercials and enough on-air talking that Joel would have thirty-eight minutes and forty-two seconds of free time. There was even a counter on the CD player that would let Joel know how much time he had left.

Using CDs like this wouldn't have been possible if Joel had been working another time slot. But there were very few people, especially farmers, who were awake from midnight till four AM so Joel could get away with it. The building from which KROW was transmitting was not very large. If the phone started ringing, or rather if the lights on the panel started blinking, Joel could hot-foot it back to the sound booth to answer the call. Almost every room in the building had a "mirror-light" (one that would blink if the panel light started blinking.) There was even a mirror-light in the john.

"Java don't fail me now!" Joel said as he headed for the coffeemaker. When he first went to work at KROW Joel hated the bitter, black stuff. Now, he couldn't survive without it. He poured a steaming hot slug of coffee into his favorite mug – "Forget Texas, Don't Mess With My Coffee!" – and added two heaping spoonfuls of sugar to the brew. He had already decided to spend the next half hour at his favorite pastime: perusing the station's old vinyl records.

At one time, this building had been the home of a soft rock/easy listening station and that was just the kind of music Joel favored and collected. In the back rooms, there were piles and piles of boxes containing vinyl records that dated all the way back to the sixties. Joel would go into a room, drag a box into one of the rooms with a mirror light, and then dig through the box to see if there was anything worth salvaging. So far, he had found some ancient Beatles, a couple of early Mommas and the Poppas and a first release recording of the Jackson Five, all of which he added to his collection.

The tired DJ decided to spend this particular thirty minutes looking through a box he had pulled from one of the most remote rooms in the station. This box looked as if it hadn't been disturbed for years. Some of the records would be broken, some warped, others would be scratched to the point of being worthless, but there might be something special in there.

Joel hadn't been able to go through the box when he first found it. He had accidentally come across the cardboard treasure chest. The backroom he had been stumbling through was so old and unused there wasn't a working light bulb in the overhead fixture. In the dark, trying to search by flashlight, Joel knocked over a box of albums. While bending down to pick up the records and put them back, Joel spotted the corner of the older box sticking out from behind a rack of ancient electronic equipment.

That night, in the moment of discovery, he had a special feeling about this bunch of records. Excited, he dragged the box of albums all the way back to the control booth. Just as he sat down and started to look through the old albums, though, the phone rang. It was his favorite radio groupie, Wanda (or was it "Wanna"?) She called in every now and then. She was one of the very few after-midnight listeners that Joel could call "regulars." She loved to tell him, in explicit language, what she wanted to do to him and what she wanted him to do to her. She was probably sixty-five and weighed over three hundred pounds but that's not the way Joel imagined her. To him, Wanda was young and svelte and built for speed. Needless to say, Mr. Fox forgot all about the box of old records for the rest of the night. After Wanda's call, he slipped it under the control board in the sound booth and prayed that no one would find it till his next shift. They hadn't. The box was where he had left it, covered with cobwebs and dust, and he pulled it into the light.

Joel took a sip from his coffee cup and glanced at the message board – no calls tonight. He'd have plenty of time to leisurely go through the records. He flipped through album after album; nothing seemed particularly interesting until he came across an album cover that was totally black. He pulled it from the box and inspected it carefully. Neither side had any writing on them, not even raised black letters, and the three enclosed edges were also blank. No logos, no trademarks, no identification numbers, no production company names. Nothing.

This was getting interesting.

"Maybe it's a white album by the Seltaeb," Joel thought.

"I'm glad I only thought that and didn't try to say it out loud," Joel spoke into the empty sound booth.

Taking out the record – there was no record sleeve – Joel looked at the record label. It was also totally black except for five words on one side written in what looked like ink made of crushed diamonds. It read "*The Damsel and the Dragon.*"

Joel looked up at the counter on the CD player. About twenty minutes was left on the CD and he decided to give this baby a listen. When he first began his midnight treasure hunts he knew he would need some way to listen to the albums he found. A scratched record is worthless. He had rummaged around in the storerooms until he found an old record player and he listened to the albums with headphones.

That was the only way to really listen to music and truly judge the quality of the recording: a good set of headphones. Joel always used a set of phones that he'd come across in an old junk store where he'd been "mining" for records. The first music he'd heard through those headphones was Roza's "King of Kings," "El Cid," and that incredible opening sequence to "The Robe." The album had been sold for a profit years ago but the headphones had stayed.

Joel put on the headphones, cued up the album, and leaned back in his chair to listen to "*The Damsel and the Dragon.*" The music began softly, sounding sort of menacing. It was a well orchestrated piece that started with a lone trumpet and slowly added violins, low brass, and timpani. As he listened, Joel's eyes kind of . . . clouded over with an eldritch mist.

"Shit! Must be getting sleepy. And I've still got five and a half hours to go!"

Joel yawned wide, closing his eyes and stretching. He finished the muscle tingling stretch by reaching up and squeezing the bridge of his nose between his thumb and forefinger.

When he opened his eyes, Joel nearly swallowed his tongue.

The sound booth had dramatically changed. Joel seemed to be in a huge cave, lit here and there by patches of fire. Not ten feet in front of him was one of the most beautiful women he had ever seen in his life. She was chained to a stake, her arms extending up above her head. She was hanging slackly, obviously unconscious, but Joel could still tell that she was someone to dream about – a lush body and blonde hair that fell almost to her waist. She was barely wearing some sort of a dull white robe-thing and what she did have on was partially ripped; Joel saw the hint of some extraordinary curves.

"Where am I?" Joel asked out loud as he stood up. ("Wait a minute, was I already standing?")

"You are in my cave, fool," said a deep, rumbling voice from above and behind him. The music played on and Joel still wore the headphones but he had plainly heard the voice, almost as if it had been recorded on the album.

Startled by the voice, Joel whirled around and looked upwards – directly into the face of an enormous lizard. The thing's eyes were easily a foot across and looked like the biggest cat's eyes that Joel had ever seen. In the light given off by the patches of fire, its skin was reddish brown, like old bricks. There were horns on the top of its head and six-inch teeth sticking out of the mouth that seemed to be the source of the response to what Joel thought was a rhetorical question.

Joel let out a scream that echoed off the walls; he whirled around and took off running. Milliseconds later, he fell over the console and somersaulted into the studio door, losing the headphones in the process.

He found himself out of the cave and back in the radio station.

"What the hell?" Joel said, wincing as he got to his feet. Everything seemed to be back to normal, if a little messy as a result of his fall. His chair was thrown over on its back, the console was a mess of CDs and paperwork, and the headphones were sitting on the floor. There was a sore spot on Joel's thigh where he had run, full tilt, hitting the console and he could feel a welt on his forehead where he had banged his head on the top of his desk.

"Damn! What the hell was that?" Joel thought, "Did I fall asleep or something?"

118

Joel pulled his chair back up and sat down, rubbing his thigh and shaking his head. He was a little disoriented and was trying very hard to figure out what had happened to him. After a few minutes he felt better but he was still very confused about what had caused the most vivid dream or hallucination he had ever had.

He checked the time, saw that he still had about eleven minutes, and began cleaning up the console. Joel had to laugh over this whole thing but, as he started to, the studio became small and closed in and the laugh turned into more of a nervous cackle than a humor-induced chuckle.

"This is crazy," he said out loud. Then he thought, "I must have fallen asleep and the music caused me to dream some dragon slayer kind of dream or something. I sort of recall a movie that had a soundtrack that kind of sounded like that and the damn thing had a dragon in it. That must have been it."

Sighing, Joel got back to cleaning up his mess. In the midst of restacking the CDs, he noticed that the music was still coming out of the headphones on the floor. Leaning over in his chair, Joel reached down to pick up the phones and froze – a piercing scream sounded from the headset!

Bounding up from his chair, Joel moved so that the console was between him and the headphones. He had a wild look in his eyes and for a second he felt like running out of the booth. But for some crazy reason, standing there, Joel's mind was drawn back to the figure of the woman chained to the big stake. His mind was racing, trying to come up with some logical, sane answer to what was going on when a second, more desperate scream issued out of the earbuds.

Then, without considering what he was doing, Joel stepped deliberately around the console, stooped over, picked up the headphones and settled them back over his ears.

He was immediately back in the cave. There, in front of him, the huge dragon, easily sixty feet long, was sitting on its haunches, intent on the woman chained to the stake. She was awake now and writhing desperately doing everything she could to get out of the chains. The dragon was leaning towards her, thick saliva dripping from his gaping maw, and regarding her like a starving pit bull might look at a hunk of raw meat. As Joel watched, the huge beast actually began rubbing its claws together.

Quickly sizing up his surroundings, Joel saw that he was in a sandy floored cave with a few mounds of rock sticking up here and there. If all of this wasn't weird enough, some of the rock, to include the ceiling and the walls, was actually on fire. Joel had no idea how he could be standing there without collapsing in a heap. This much fire combined with the heavy armor he was wearing would surely have resulted in him being overcome . . .

"Wait a minute; I'm wearing armor?"

Joel looked down and, sure enough, he was wearing full plate mail, just like he had seen in movies and books all of his life. Strapped to his left arm was a large, wooden shield that was rimmed in gold and in his right hand was a long, skinny sword with a big, blue gem in the . . .

"That's the pommel," Joel thought, "And how did I know that's what you call it?"

He also vaguely remembered standing in another dark chamber (not a cave though) in front of an old man with long, white hair and a long, white beard and having the old man tell him that the *feuerschild* would protect him from the "dragon's breath." He pulled the sword up in front of him and even though it was made of steel or something like it the thing felt as light as a feather! The fact that it was glowing white and giving off cold mist didn't even faze Joel – the weird meter was already pegged so far to the right that Joel figured a glowing, misty white sword was par for the course.

As he moved the sword to an *en garde* position ("A WHAT position?"), Joel centered his concentration back on the dragon. The huge lizard still hadn't noticed him and the young woman was a little too preoccupied with her captor to check out the rest of the cave.

"Now, my dear," rumbled the huge beast, "let us see what delicious treats await my evening meal."

With that, the dragon reached out with its enormous, claw. The girl froze, the expression on her face clearly revealing the sheer terror of the horrific fate that awaited her. Her eyes, bluer than a mountain sky, grew wide as she watched the great claw moving toward her. It was obvious that the evil lizard was going to rip what little clothing remained about the damsel's form so he (it?) could gawk at her nakedness before he cut her to pieces with his razor-sharp teeth.

120

"I WOULD NOT DO THAT IF I WERE YOU!" shouted Joel, clanging his sword against a clump of burning rock. The sword hissed, spewed forth a cloud of mist, and the rock split in two, the fire instantly extinguished.

At the first sound of Joel's voice, the dragon whipped its head around, focusing its horrible gaze on the young knight ("yeah, I guess that's what I am.")

"Well, you brainless oaf," spit the dragon, "have you made up your mind? Are you a disappearing wizard or a knight of folly, come to seek your death?"

"I am neither, worm," retorted Joel, "I started tonight as a disc jockey and it's time for me to spin the song of your death." ("Not bad . . . especially if I live to tell about this.")

"Whatever you are, you are trespassing and interrupting my dinner. But there's nothing wrong with a little entertainment to work up my appetite!"

Without hesitation, the dragon lunged toward one of the piles of burning rock and, opening its jaws, bit off a large portion of the burning pile. Turning towards Joel, it opened its mouth wide and spewed out a stream of fire and smoke! Not even thinking, Joel crouched down and placed the shield he was carrying between his body and the flames. Fire crashed into the shield but the temperature behind the shield didn't go up a single degree – Joel was completely unharmed by the dragon's breath!

Rising up, Joel saw the dragon looking at him with a malevolent stare.

"So, I see you have a toy. Well, little boy," the dragon spat, "let us see if you know how to use it!"

The giant beast, stalking Joel like a jungle cat might approach a wary antelope, moved to its right, obviously trying to get behind the warrior's shield. Joel mirrored the beast's movements, keeping the shield between them while he tried to think of what his next step should be.

Suddenly, the dragon's mouth opened again. It bit off a large portion of the burning wall, and then whipping back towards Joel, the great beast blew flaming death at him. Joel, once again, crouched low and the mass of flames burst against the shield. The fire blew out and just as Joel looked over the top of the shield he saw the great lizard running at him, intending to bowl him over and either grapple with him or destroy the young hero's protection.

Throwing himself to his left, Joel barely avoided the dragon's charge and with great effort, got his right arm up with the sword. The dragon roared in pain as the white sword bounced along the scales on the dragon's flank. It left white streaks of frost everywhere it touched the enormous creature.

Skittering to a stop, the dragon again crunched down on a pile of the burning rocks and faced Joel. This time, Joel barely got the shield up in time to prevent his goose from being dragon-fried.

Joel figured the dragon would try another charge so he quickly looked up and took a fighting stance as the flames stopped. Instead, the dragon was picking up a boulder with its great front paws.

"Let me see if you can catch boulders with that shield of yours," chuckled the dragon. And he let the rock fly!

It crashed against Joel's shield and the full force of the stone smashed against Joel's arm, forcing him back against the wall of the cave. The dragon had him trapped against the wall and defenseless against the thrown boulders. Again and again, the huge beast threw rocks at the young knight and each time Joel either avoided them or took the brunt of the assault against the shield. Before long, the shield began to crack and splinter and Joel knew that his lot was up.

The dragon laughed as the broken shield fell away from Joel's arm. His prey was now completely at his mercy!

"Ah, ha, ha, ha! Now feel the full flames of my wrath, puny mortal!"

Then stretching up to its full height, the enormous beast reached its scaly neck up to the roof, it's jaws open to bite off a huge mouthful of the burning rock.

At that moment, Joel summoned up his last bit of strength and his final ounce of courage and ran towards the dragon. Joel thrust his icy sword into the demon's chest, exposed when it lifted its head.

The end of the evil beast was something to behold. Squirming about, the death throes of the creature nearly accomplished what its cruel intent had been. Joel avoided the thrashing body, waiting till the beast was totally still, and then retrieved his sword from the breast of the beast.

Limping over to the maiden, who had fainted again, Joel raised up his sword with one arm and, cleaving the chains with a single stroke, he caught the woman's limp body with his other arm. Dropping the sword, he held her gently and stroked her hair back from her lovely face. As he held her, the young woman's eyes fluttered open and her lips widened into a beautiful smile.

"Oh, my lord, you are my hero! How can I ever thank you! My father, King Everett, will surely want to reward you as well! Oh, hold me closer; I still shake from fear at the thought of what that evil dragon had in store for me!"

Joel couldn't think of a single thing to say; he just smiled.

The music had stopped; when Joel reached up to pull off the headphones, he felt nothing but the steel of his helmet. It was obvious to him now: listening to the music from the record had transported him to this new and different world. It wasn't the old headphones or the exotically decorated album; it was the power of the music itself.

As someone who had spent his life working around music, collecting it, enjoying it, Joel had always believed that songs and melodies had the ability to affect your life, maybe even change it. Now he had tangible proof of that power.

For a moment, he wondered how he would ever get back to the world he knew. Then, looking down into the beautiful eyes of his princess and seeing her smile up at him, he didn't care.

*   *   *   *   *

"Dang his hide! Where is he?"

The owner of KROW and the station manager had just broken into the booth and their DJ, Joel Fox, was nowhere in sight. Not only that, the booth looked worse than it did after a tornado had come within a hundred feet of the place back in 1989. And there, in the middle of the floor, looking like it had been broken in two, stomped on and then set on fire, were Joel's headphones.

"I've looked everywhere," said the station manager, "the bathrooms, the kitchen, the storage rooms, even out back in the yard, and he ain't anywhere!"

"I'll kill him!" screamed the owner, "we've had nothing but dead air goin' out for the last hour and I didn't hire that jack-ass to go runnin' off in the middle of the night!"

"Do you think we ought to call the police? This place looks like someone came in here and dragged him out by his heels. You don't think there's some foul play involved here, do you?"

"Oh, I'm going to call the cops, all right, but it'll be to find his butt and drag him back here to pay for the damages before I fire him! And get something on the air before another minute goes by! What's he got in the CD player?"

The station manager went over to the console and started pushing buttons and shoving papers and CD cases out of the way to try and make sense out of the mess. Finally, the CD tray on one of the machines popped open.

"This is weird," said the manager, "I've never seen a CD like this."

The disc that the station manager held up to the light was jet black with nothing but some weird silvery writing on one side.

"Well put it on the air! I don't want another second of dead air going out."

As the owner started to walk to his office to call the police, he suddenly had second thoughts about putting out anything that had been chosen by a jockey so irresponsible that he would tear the place up and then take off. He turned around and walked back towards the booth just as the station manager was pushing the CD tray closed.

"What's the name of the CD anyway"?

"It must be some kind of soundtrack," said the station manager as the music began to swell from the playback speakers, "it's called *Attack of the Goblin Horde*."

The Mayan Project
By Pamala A. Williams
©2009

"Last bolt's in," Stan Trevino said.

Mikayla McGovern turned from her perusal of the Earth, sitting low in the sky. Looking through the visor of the NASA-issued space suit, she watched the workmen gather up tools and walk away from the just-completed dome.

"Start the atmosphere machine. Let's make sure there are no leaks."

Stan signaled to one of the workmen and looked back at her.

"How long do we test it?"

"If there are no leaks, then we'll start moving things in an hour."

Stan nodded and looked at the time display on the back of his glove. The time was still set on Earth's Eastern Standard Time. They hadn't yet figured out how to tell time on the moon. He supposed it didn't matter anyway. Stan made his way back to the dome. He'd stay with it for an hour checking for leaks. He'd get Tom and Ross to stay with him and send the other guys back to the lunar module.

Mikayla went back to the module and sat at her desk. She had paperwork that needed to be done. There was always paperwork.

"Is it finished, yet?" asked Jeannie Sunderland. Jeannie was the communications officer.

Mikayla nodded. "Could you get Colonel Shanks for me?"

Jeannie turned to the com-board and started doing her job.

"You got something for me, Mike?" asked the colonel over the com. Mikayla could see the colonel and knew he could see her. She just hoped she looked better than she felt. Six months on the moon had taken its toll. She needed to be back on the Earth. She needed to breathe fresh air. She needed…something.

"Last bolt went in, Sir. We're testing it to make sure there are no leaks. If all goes well, we'll start moving in in about an hour."

"Excellent. Keep me informed. How's the landing strip coming?"

"Good. We should have it finished by the end of the week."

"Step it up, Mike, I need it by tomorrow."

Mikayla was incredulous. "Tomorrow? No offense, Colonel, but are you out of your friggin' mind? We still have the ramp to finish and install the lights. My people have been working ten hours a day on that landing strip for months without a day off."

"Tomorrow, Mike. No negotiations. Do what ya gotta do. To quote a hero of mine, 'Make it so'."

Mikayla rolled her eyes. "I can't promise anything, Colonel, but I'll do my best. You got something coming in?"

"Somebody," he corrected. "Jake Blackriver and his crew, to get started on the excavations."

"Good. I was wondering when they'd be showing up."

"Had to have a place to keep them, and now with the dome completed…"

"Hey now, wait a minute. That dome was supposed to be used to house my people. We've been living out of these crappy temp shelters for six months. My people deserve that dome. We worked hard for it."

"Now don't get your panties in a wad, Mike. There's room for all of you in it."

"How many people is Blackriver bringing?"

"He's bringing in thirty this go round, more later."

"Colonel, the dome is not gonna be big enough for all of our equipment plus my people and his people."

"So you all become really close friends. And after you get a new shipment next week, you can start on your second dome."

"Colonel, my people were going to start on Halston's crater next week."

"So, split up your team, half on Halston's and half on the new dome."

"And this time next year we'll still be waiting for something to get finished. Colonel, couldn't Blackriver and his bunch take over the crappy temp shelters? They could even move them closer to the excavation site."

"Those crappy temp shelters are to be dismantled and returned on the next ship out. Just deal with it, Mike."

Mikayla set her jaw. "I need more people. Now, I don't have room for them."

"Deal with it. Shanks out." And the screen went blank.

"Aaaaahhh!" Mikayla was livid. "Bureaucrats!" She dropped her head into her hands.

"Could be worse," Jeannie said.

Mikayla swung her head around to look at Jeannie. "And just how could this be worse?"

"He could be coming himself for an inspection."

"Don't even think that," Mikayla remonstrated. "That's not even remotely funny."

"Wasn't meant to be. You know he's been threatening to come up here for months, now."

"He seems satisfied with the pictures we're sending him."

"So far. But you know he's gonna want a first-hand look."

"Let's hope he waits until we've got another dome ready."

Stan came in just then. "No detectable leaks, Mike. Ready to start moving in."

Mikayla nodded. "Let's get everyone to chow. I've got some announcements."

Stan nodded and went to spread the word.

* * * * *

Mikayla stood in front of the lunar map on the wall as she called for attention. "People, I've got some announcements. First, the dome is finished and holding atmosphere." There were a number of cheers. Mikayla smiled and went on. "We need to get moved out of these temp quarters and into the dome as soon as possible. Second, we've got to finish the landing strip yesterday. We've got the excavating crew due in here tomorrow."

"Tomorrow? Mike, that's impossible. We can't get that ramp finished by tomorrow, let alone install all the lights. Why can't they just parachute or whatever like they've been dropping our supplies?" asked Brad Taylor. "Or better yet, wait until next week?"

"If they're gonna be here tomorrow, that means that they're already on their way, so there's no waiting for next week. Believe me, I'm as pissed as you. I want every one of you on the strip. Stan, your people will start on the lights. Brad, do what you can. I told the Colonel that it couldn't be done, but he wants it, so we're going to try to deliver."

The men and women on the crew grumbled and groaned.

"Third, Jake Blackriver is bringing thirty people on his excavating crew. And they're staying with us in the dome."

"Thirty people? Mike, the dome's not that big." Bob Townsend was on his feet, waving his hands in the air. "Let's just give them these crappy things we've been living in."

"Yeah, if we're moving into the dome, these shelters will be available. They can have these," someone else said.

"Fourth," Mikayla continued. "These crappy temp shelters are to be dismantled and loaded up on the next ship out. They're going back to NASA. Per the Colonel. Period."

"That stinks, and you know it, Mike."

"Yeah, the excavation crew could use these 'til we get the next dome built," someone else said.

"Guys, I'm just like you, I have to follow orders, too. I tried to argue with the Colonel, but his mind was made up. His exact words were 'Deal with it.' That's what we have to do. We have to deal with it. I don't like it any more than you do. But that's the way it is."

She looked around at the people who were doing their best to make a colony on the moon. God, she loved these people. She handpicked each and every one. They were the best of what they did. It just didn't seem fair to have Blackriver and his bunch usurp everything they've worked for.

"Fifth. We're getting a shipment in next week. We'll be starting on a new dome to house all of us more comfortably. I know that we were going to start on the Halston's crater, but we've got to have more room. I need to bring up more people, and I've got to have a place for them. The sooner we can get the new dome finished, the sooner we can bring up the next batch of workers. If we're all working on the dome, it'll be finished a lot quicker than this one was. I know the colonel expects us to start on Halston's Crater, but that's just going to have to wait. We need more room as soon as possible. He'll just have to deal with it."

There were cheers throughout the dining hall.

She looked around. "Any questions?"

*   *   *   *   *

By the time the shuttle arrived the next day, the lights were lit half-way down one side of the strip, and the ramp was not quite finished. But the shuttle landed safely. The shuttle crew and Blackriver and his men were shown to the dome.

"You're Mike McGovern?" asked Jake Blackriver. "Sorry, I thought you were a man."

"You don't think a woman can run a construction crew? You don't think a woman can start a colony on the moon? You don't think a woman can….."

"Whoa, not so fast. I was just told your name was Mike. Mike is a guy's name. Just some misunderstanding. For your information, my mother is the president of Watkins University in Connecticut. So, I have nothing against women in positions of power, or whatever. Where do you want us?"

Mikayla knew exactly where she wanted him and his men, but declined to say so. "Get with Stan. He's been assigning quarters. We're a little cramped, so until the new dome gets built, we're going to have to get real friendly."

"I thought a new dome was just finished. What gives?"

"This is the new dome. It also happens to be the only dome at the moment. We won't get started on the next one until we get the supplies next week. We've spent the last six months building this dome and the landing strip. We still have a few days left on the landing strip."

"Will it be ready for us to takeoff," asked Captain Harris. Jonathan Harris was the shuttle captain. He and his crew of six were to take the dismantled temp shelters back to NASA.

"We'll have it ready. You gonna dismantle the temp shelters?"

"That's what we're supposed to do."

"No problem, then. Blackriver, when are you going to get started on the excavation?"

"Plan on starting tomorrow, if that pleases you," Jake was starting to wonder what he had gotten his crew into. Was she trying to be a bitch? If so, she was doing a good job.

Mikayla sighed. "Look, I'm sorry if I seem a bit abrupt. I've been under a lot of pressure, lately, and the colonel throwing things at me has me a bit unsettled. Give me a day or so to get used to the new situation and I'll be back to my normal self."

Whatever that is, she thought.

Whatever that is, Jake thought.

"Anyway, if I can be of any assistance to you, let me know. I really wasn't expecting you guys until next week, at the earliest, so things are not as ready as they would have been. Feel free to explore the dome. The sleeping quarters are marked by a number on the door. Stan will let you know the room number that you are assigned. Captain, I hope your crew doesn't mind sharing a room. We are cramped, here."

"We'll be fine, as long as we've got a place to sleep where we're not weightless." He smiled, and so did Mikayla. She remembered trying to sleep on the shuttle to the moon. The feeling was just too weird for words.

"Well then, let me show you to the Dining Hall." As Mikayla led the way through the dome to the Dining Hall, Travis Proffitt ran toward her with a hand full of papers.

"What's up?"

"Just got the monitors on-line, and it shows a small meteor coming this way." He held out the papers so she could see the reports.

"Do you think it's going to hit the surface? It could pass by and on toward Earth."

"It's too close to tell, right now. If it does pass us by, no biggie. It's small enough to burn up in Earth's atmosphere, but if it hits the surface, it's big enough to cause some major damage."

Mikayla rubbed her forehead. "OK. Tell Jeannie to call in the crews. Can't have them exposed if one's going to hit the area. Keep an eye on it. I'll be in the monitor room in a little while."

Travis nodded and turned to hurry away to the communications room.

"God, I hope it misses us."

"You've had other hits since you've been here?" asked Jake.

Mikayla nodded. "Not many, but one is too many. The closest one was about two miles away. It took two weeks for the dust to settle. Had us all crapping our drawers waiting to see where it landed."

Jake had actually never considered the threat of meteors crashing to the surface of the moon while he was working on it. The thought was very frightening. He was glad that he was going to be mostly working underground.

*   *   *   *   *

The lunar inhabitants kept a watchful eye on the pending disaster. A few hours later, the meteor hit. Luckily it was off its mark by one hundred some miles.

That disaster averted, everyone went back to work.

*   *   *   *   *

Three days later, the temp shelters had been dismantled and loaded onto the shuttle. The ramp was not quite finished, but it was finished enough that the shuttle had no problem taking off. The lights were almost caught up with the ramp. One more day, and it would all be done.

Jake Blackriver and his crew had started excavating in the side of the crater, making a cave-like entrance big enough to get equipment in to start the dig down into the bowels of the moon. That was where most of the colony was going to be. This had to be big enough to house a lot of people. It had to be big enough to house a lot of industry. People were going to be living and working on the moon for quite some time.

Jake didn't know why, he was hired to do a job, and, well hey, not everyone gets to go to the moon to work. He couldn't resist a challenge. Especially one like this. Why they wanted to put a colony on the moon was anybody's guess, but he had an interesting job and he was going to do the best he could. He was excited to be here, and with luck, he'd even eventually be able to get along with Mike. Not that he was holding out any hope. She was a little too hostile to suit him. Besides, there were other women here. He'd make friends. And if not, well, he'd try celibacy. Maybe.

Jake knocked on Mikayla's office door.

"Come in." He heard the muffled command through the door, and entered. Mikayla was sitting at her desk shuffling through some papers while staring at her computer screen.

"You wanted to see me?"

Mikayla looked up and motioned him to one of the chairs in front of her desk.

"Please take a seat." She put the papers down and sat back in her chair. "Mr. Blackriver, I…"

"Jake. Call me Jake."

Mikayla nodded. "Jake, I think we got off to a bad start. We had just completed this dome after working on it for six long months. Before we could even got moved in, I was told that you and your crew were on your way. I was then told that you would be sharing the dome with us. You notice how there's not a lot of unused space here. I was going to bring up another group of workers, now I have no place to put them. I was pretty pissed off."

"Yeah, I can understand how that would piss you off. But where did you think we would live?"

"To be honest, I thought you would take the temp shelters we'd been living in and move them closer to the excavation site. As you got some of the building completed, you'd move in there while you worked on more of it."

"Well, that does make a little sense. Okay, I understand why you were pissed. Especially if it was thrown at you all of a sudden. We okay now?"

Mikayla smiled. "We're okay. As long as you keep a good hand on your crew."

"No problem. They're a pretty good bunch of guys. As long as they don't get drunk. Then all bets are off," he smiled.

She smiled again. "No problem there, we don't have any liquor on the moon."

Jake's eyebrows went up. "No booze? How do you keep a construction crew happy with no booze?"

"Just keep them working until they drop."

"That's not quite fair, is it? I mean, all work and no play makes for a very restless crew."

"I know. But we don't have a lot of time to worry about enjoying ourselves. We're under the gun. We've only got a few years to get this thing done. Speaking of which, how far down are you?"

Jake looked at her. He wasn't supposed to report to her, was he? He searched his memory, and couldn't remember exactly what Colonel Shanks had told him. Something about the project manager. He figured that guy was back on Earth.

"Well, if you need to know, I'm still widening the cavern to get all our equipment in. Should start sinking the shaft next week sometime."

Mikayla couldn't believe it. This man had a crew of thirty. He had all the latest equipment available, and hadn't started sinking the shaft after working for nearly a week.

"Jake, that shaft should be a least ten to twenty feet down, by now. We have deadlines. You need to keep to your deadlines."

"What deadlines? I was told to come up here, do my job, and keep the project manager happy. Whoever he is."

Mikayla sighed. "I am the project manager, and I am not happy. I'll print out a copy of the deadlines for you so you can try to keep to them. If this job isn't ready in time, I don't even want to think about the consequences."

"What consequences. If it's not finished, we keep working until it is. No big deal. It'll be finished."

"Do you even know why you're here?" Mikayla asked.

"Cause I'm good at what I do. They want some excavations done a la Cheyenne Mountain, and I can deliver. On Earth or on the Moon."

"Do you know what this project is called?"

"Yeah. The Mayan Project. Although I don't think the Mayan's were from the moon. Nor do I think they lived in underground complexes."

"You have no idea of what's going on, then?" Mikayla couldn't believe Colonel Shanks hadn't told him of the magnitude of this project and the reasons behind it.

"Some big wig wants a colony on the moon. I suppose it's like a stepping stone to get more exploration done on Mars. What's the big deal. I'm working, getting paid, quite handsomely I might add, and Mr. Big Shot gets his underground city."

Mikayla rose from her chair and went to the filing cabinet. She took a file from it and flipped through the file until she found a large photograph. She handed the photograph to Jake.

"Do you know what that is?"

Jake looked that the photo. "Let me guess, the Mayan Calendar?"

Mikayla took the photo and placed it back in the file. She laid the file on her desk.

"The Mayan calendar ends on December 10, 2012. Five years from now. Do you know why?"

Jake shook his head. Who knew what Mayans did. They were all dead, weren't they?

"Neither do we. But it ends quite abruptly. That calendar is millennia old. Why end it then?"

Jake moved to answer, but Mikayla cut him off.

"We think that they thought that the world would end on that date, so they didn't bother to go any further with their calendar. What would be the point? The world basically came to an end around 60 billion years ago when a meteor or small asteroid hit the Earth killing off all the dinosaurs. We think something like that will happen again."

"On December 10, 2012."

"Exactly. Why do you think Reagan built Star Wars?"

"That was actually built? I thought it was a joke."

"No. President Reagan had an astrologist that he consulted daily. He knew that there was a very strong possibility that we could be bombarded with meteors and asteroids. He devised a way to help prevent that by sending up the Star Wars satellite. He wanted to leave something behind to help save the Earth. He knew he would never live to see the destruction, when it came."

"I know that there's the Asteroid Belt and sometimes they collide with one another and get shot out of their orbits and hurtle through space to collide with whatever gets in their path. And that Earth has been hit several times in the past. I had no idea that Reagan's hare-brained idea was actually implemented."

"It was actually a very smart idea. Although given the times, I can understand how Russia and China would think we were actually aiming the warheads at them. But it wasn't enough. What we are doing is not just building a colony on the moon. We are hoping to preserve man-kind. By the first of January 2012, we will begin shuttling people up here. By September, we will start bringing up world leaders. So when December 10th comes, there will be a lot of people safely ensconced in our underground city."

"And what happens if whatever's going to end life on Earth hits the moon first?"

"That's not in the equation."

"Not in the equation? Why the hell not?" Jake got out of his chair and was pacing up and down the small office space.

"How many people are we talking about bringing up here? A couple of thousand?"

"Closer to ten to fifteen thousand."

"Mike, there are over six billion people on Earth. What about everyone else? Did you think about them?"

"Of course, I've thought about them. My God, do you think I'm some kind of monster? I don't want to leave anyone behind. At all, but we don't have enough time to make enough underground cities to house them all. I'd love to, but there's not enough time."

"Why wasn't something done a long time ago? If we've known about the Mayan prophecy for a while, how come we're just now doing something about it? Can you tell me that?"

"I've been working on this project since I was fourteen and found out about the calendar and its implications. It was my main objective in college to learn as much as possible to get this off the ground. As soon as I graduated high school, I contacted the people who needed to get this started. It took me years, years before anyone would take me seriously. It took a while before technology allowed us the hope that this could happen. Then, we had to have funding. I have never stopped working on this project since I was fourteen years old. I have not had a life, only this project. So excuse me if I'm a little centered on this colony."

Jake sat back down in his chair. My God but there was lot for him to think about. He prayed that the Mayan dude that made the calendar just got tired of working on it and quit. He didn't want to think of what Mike had just proposed.

*   *   *   *   *

Lights flashed and warning buzzers screamed all through the facility. Jeannie notified all outside crews to take cover. Jake locked down the excavation so no one went outside. Mikayla paced back and forth in view of the monitors. Travis Proffit pounded keys in front of one monitor, then rolled his chair to the next one and began pounding the keyboard of that monitor.

"Let's have it."

Travis looked up at Mikayla. She saw him visibly swallow the lump in his throat. "Uh, looks like about a dozen or so coming this way."

Mikayla's eyes grew large. "A dozen?"

Travis nodded. "Or so."

Mikayla closed her eyes for a couple of seconds. "How soon?"

"Uh, fifteen, thirty minutes."

"Travis, we need more warning. This can't work. We've got crews working in three different craters. It'll take them longer than that just to reach safety. We need more warning."

"I agree, Mike, but we don't have any sensors out farther than that. We need more sensors. We need to put some on the dark side. If we had some there, we could get a lot more warning. We could even keep an eye on the belt and maybe get something up here in time to avert a major disaster. Until then, this is all we've got."

Mikayla turned on her heel and ran to the communications room.

"Get me Shanks, NOW!"

Jeannie dropped the pencil she was holding and started the link to Houston.

"What's up, Mike?" asked Colonel Shanks a few minutes later.

"What's up? We're about to be bombarded by a dozen meteors and no time to get to shelter, with nothing to protect ourselves from annialation. Other than that, just wanted to say hello."

Shanks sighed. "Damn. I was hoping we had more time. I got a crew headed your way, now. We've been working on a meteor cannon, and are sending the prototype your way. We want to test it and makes sure it does what we want it to. If so, we'll make more."

"Can it get here in fifteen minutes?"

"Sorry, Mike, it hasn't docked with the space station, yet. It'll be tomorrow at the earliest."

"Then tell the crew to expect the worst. We're not sure where they're gonna land. Alert the station that they could be headed there, too."

"I'll start getting supplies together to make repairs, just in case. It'll be a few days before we have a launch window."

"If they hit us dead on, there won't be anything to repair. We need more sensors, Colonel. We need a lot more. Travis wants to put some on the dark side. We need sensors and towers. And we need them yesterday. We also need more men to erect them. My people are spread too thin as it is."

"I'll be coming up with this new shipment. I want a first-hand look."

"About time. We've been expecting you for three years."

"Yeah, well, duty calls, couldn't seem to get away. But now, it looks like duty is calling me to the moon. I'll see you soon, Mike."

"I hope so, Colonel, I really hope so. Mike out."

The main complex had dodged the bullet, but Crater Seven had sustained a direct hit. It was lucky that it wasn't completed, but the damage was almost total. They'd have to clear the wreckage and start from scratch. Crater Five sustained some damage, but was repairable. A dust cloud hung over the area making visibility difficult. The shuttle landed, but it was dicey. Several meteors had passed the moon, one took out a small communications satellite before crashing to Earth. By the time it hit the Earth, it had burned enough off to be relatively small. Unfortunately, it landed in the middle of a small town in the outback of Australia and essentially destroyed the entire town. Only those living a few miles from the town survived. The headlines throughout the world read "Round One – Nature".

Mikayla met Colonel Harris as he entered the dome with the rest of the Shuttle crew. "Colonel, good to see you."

"Likewise, Mike, likewise. Wasn't sure what to expect when we got here. Your communications have not been clear."

"Sorry. We're running about half power until the solar panels have been replaced that were damaged in the meteor storm. Glad to hear about your promotion."

Colonel Harris grinned. "So was my wife." Colonel Harris looked around at the hustle and bustle of the center. "You got a place picked out for the meteor cannon?"

"Jake, Travis, Stan, Brad and I have been going over maps of the area trying to figure out strategic places for the cannons. I've got the area mapped out in my office. How many cannons do you think we'll get?"

"We brought up one, but we've got fifty in production right now. Hopefully, they'll work. If so, we're going to station some on Earth as well."

Mikayla nodded. She knew that if the meteors got past them on the moon, that the Earth cannons wouldn't be much help.

*   *   *   *   *

When Colonel Shanks arrived the following week, he brought two more meteor cannons with him as well as repair supplies, and towers, sensors, and ten people to help get them erected and set. He was glad there was not as much damage as there could have been, but was upset that there was as much damage as there was.

"When do we move all this stuff underground?" he asked.

"We start moving in as soon as we get back on-line one-hundred percent. Should be tomorrow. We've been moving most of the equipment since the last meteor storm."

"Good, best be underground as soon as possible. Don't want a repeat of the last one."

"They're coming more frequently, and more at a time. This last one was the worst, so far."

"How are the animals doing?"

"So far, so good. Jake has a crew excavating to each of the craters for safety exits. He plans on continuing excavations even after…"

"Yeah, well, he may have to. But let's hope not."

*   *   *   *   *

"Coming this way, Mike," Travis pointed to the monitor.

"Get the cannons ready," Mikayla yelled into a walkie-talkie. "They're on their way. Take out as many as you can."

Mikayla and Colonel Shanks stood in the command center watching the monitors. This was it. December 10, 2012. The Mayan Prophecy was about to be proven.

139

Dance, Gypsy

The full moon has come to the gypsy encampment
The horses at rest and the bonfire laid
A blanket of stars settles down o'er the wagons
And out of the night steps a bold gypsy maid

Crimson and gold is the cloth which adorns her
Flashing dark eyes and black flowing hair
Slim as a reed she stands by the fire
With one supple arm flung into the air

Sweetly at first come the instruments voices
Violins passed on for hundreds of years
Witness to all of a gypsy's great passion
Polished with many a wanderer's tears

Ever so slowly the gypsy maid dances
And circles the fire with sparks in her eyes
Then leaping and bending and whirling faster
She dances her joy for the stars in the skies

Around and about the maid spins enchantment
And even old souls are stirred by the sight
Passions run high in the heart of the gypsy
For every man here knows what happens tonight

A night of all nights is this, to be sure
When a young gypsy maid, unwooed and unwed
Loosens the braids of her childhood years
And takes for herself a lover to bed

Skillful and sure are the steps of the maiden
Instinctively knowing with all of her heart
The path she must take and the obstacles there
That keep a young girl and her lover apart

Then suddenly everything ceases to move
The violins, gone from the quiet night air
To the grass, like a stone, drops the maid by the fire
And offers her hand to the man who stands there

For this is the man she has chosen to marry
The one who has stolen the heart from her breast
A laughing dark gypsy, both gently and strong
A loving companion on life's gypsy quest
He leads her now swiftly deep into the forest
Where, soft with rose petals, the marriage bed stands
The symbol of joining throughout all the ages
Prepared by her husband with strong, loving hands

As the young maidens cry of surrender goes out
Those in the camp will hear not a sound
For the feastings begun and the revels will last
'Til the full gypsy moon sinks into the ground

Wine will flow swiftly as blood through the veins
As wild hearts sing and cry out to each other
Laughter and dancing and sweet violins
And every man here calls every man brother

So dance, gypsy, laugh, be merry and sing
Rejoice in the love found by two of our own
For tomorrow we go where the stars have decreed
But this night has seen two who shall not go alone

Wendy Easterling
© 1991

The Portal
By Kenneth King
©2009

I will try not to worry you
I have seen things that you will never see
Leave it to memory me
Don't dare me to breathe

-R.E.M.

The portal changed Mitch. He came back and wasn't the same. It was as if someone had taken him away for a brief time, turned off half of him, and then let him back loose in the world. There was no spark to him, no strength of spirit. No one could quite explain it. He was just slower.

Of course, everyone noticed it. Everyone knew that he'd gone through. But they didn't know quite what to make of it. Mitch had been curious about the portal since it had first arrived, while most everyone else was too scared to go near, and just pretended it would go away. One night he'd told Laurie he was going up to visit with it a bit. She'd fussed at him, as normal, but he'd shrugged it off. "I'm just goin' for a few minutes, I ain't gonna stay all night, promise." Mitch didn't come home that night. They'd found him the next morning, lying on the ground in front of it, his clothes and skin coated with dust.

It'd been a few weeks now, but everyone was too afraid of upsetting Laurie to talk to her about it, other than the occasional "So, how's Mitch doin'?"

"Fine, he's just fine," she'd say. Sometimes, involuntarily, she'd bite her lip after she said this. At night, Mitch would lie in bed on his side, facing away from her; sometimes he'd shiver, hard, even though it was summer; the desert nights were cool, but not intolerable, and they had sheets covering them. She'd pull up tight against his back, her arm around his side, trying to keep him warm. Eventually, the shivering would stop, but Laurie was never sure if she was the reason why.

*　　　*　　　*　　　*　　　*

142

The portal had simply been there one day. Mitch was driving back into town from the oil fields with his best friend Larry. Mitch's big, dirty Ford F250 crested the hill above the valley where the small Arizona town lay, throwing pale brown dirt and dust everywhere in its wake. Larry spotted it, off on top a nearby hill. Mitch put the truck into a hard right, the big worn tires sliding over the dirt road, before they finally caught their grip and sent the truck on its way. They pulled up a dozen yards away, and walked up to the top of the hill where the portal lay.

"What the fuck is it?" Larry asked.

"I got no idea," said Mitch. "I ain't never seen anything like it."

The portal seemed out of place in the bleached, minimalist scheme of the desert. About eight feet tall, with a thick base that tapered to a dull point at the top, it looked like someone had take a slab of white stone, like pumice, and driven it into the ground far enough that it stood upright, like a door. Except that doors generally lead somewhere, and have some sort of building around them. The portal was just there.

"Look at the pattern in it," Mitch said, pointing at something on the portal. "It's like the thing was formed that way, though, not carved at all. Like it was shaped by someone."

Larry looked at the center of the stone, where he'd seen, about chest height, the pattern Mitch had spoken of. It was just as Mitch had said. Almost like a sunburst, there were a number of deep cracks in the surface of the portal leading away from a vague circular indention in the center, all starting out as deep as the indentation, then gradually becoming shallower as they progressed outward, till each simply stopped at a point. But there were no edges, no telltale signs that someone had done this with a hammer and chisel, or a stick of dynamite. The pattern simply existed within the rock, as if it were natural.

Larry drew close and raised his hand to touch it. His fingers touched the stone briefly, sliding down across the surface, and then Larry snapped his hand away quickly. "Fuck!"

"What?" asked Mitch, then again. "*What?*"

"It's hot! Fucking thing burned my fingers!" Larry nursed his sore fingers, putting them in his mouth and sucking on them.

Mitch burst out laughing. "Thing's probably been sittin' out here all day, jackass! What were you expectin', it'd be an ice cube?"

Larry looked over at the portal warily. "Rocks don't get that hot, man, they just don't. Ain't natural. Fucking thing's gonna give me a blister, I swear."

"You're just bein' a big baby. Can't be that bad. Watch." Mitch approached the portal, and put his hand gently on it, but not before he brushed his fingers off on his jeans, and wet the tips on his tongue. He let his fingers linger in one spot for a moment, then looked at Larry. "Jesus, Larry, it feels like a fucking rock. Ain't burnin' up or nothin'. Just a damn rock. Come over here and feel it." But Larry refused. Mitch ran his hands along the sides of the portal, dragging them across the pale stone towards the pattern, tracing one of the cracks from its end to the indention in the stone's center, where he stopped his fingers. Then, slowly, his fingers sank into the surface.

"Shit!" Mitch said, pulling his hand back as fast as he could. "Did you see that?!"

"No," said Larry. "What? What was it?"

"My fingers. They went in the rock. Just started to slide in, like when you stick your hands in dough. Exact same fucking thing."

Larry looked at him for a moment, then at the pattern in the portal. "Do it again."

Hesitantly, Mitch put his fingers back in the center of the pattern, and again, his fingers started to slide into the surface, the stone seeming to soften enough to allow his fingers to force their way in. Mitch pulled them back out again quickly. "Try it," he said.

Larry put his hands in the same place, but jerked them back a moment later. "Ow! Damn thing burned me again. What the fuck?"

Mitch put his fingers back on the pattern, and once again, they slowly slid into the stone. "It's strange," he said quietly. "It's soft; like slidin' your fingers inside someone's skin."

"The hell with this," Larry said. "Let's go. We can tell someone in town about it, see what they think. They'll think we're fuckin' nuts, but we'll tell 'em anyway."

"Yeah," Mitch replied. "Man, they gotta feel this…"

"Alright then, let's go." Larry said, but Mitch didn't move; he just sat there, letting his fingers slide farther in. "Mitch. Mitch, c'mon!"

Mitch pulled his fingers out. "Okay, okay. Let's go."

*   *   *   *   *

Laurie and Mitch sat and ate dinner quietly. She'd made one of his favorite meals, chicken lasagne, but he just sat there, as if he was no longer able to tell the difference between one type of food or another. The fork or spoon just dipped into whatever was on the plate and conveyed the substance to Mitch's mouth, where it was chewed and then swallowed.

"Barb and Jim were in the store today," Laurie said. "They asked how you were doin'. I told 'em you were just fine. Barb said we should all get together one night and see a movie, or maybe get some dinner. She said that new ribs place is really tasty, and might give the Roadhouse a run for its money." Laurie looked over at Mitch. He ate another bite of the lasagne, or rather, his hand put the fork in his mouth, and then his mouth realized it was suppose to take the food and chew. Mitch didn't look at her. He just sat there with his shoulders slightly slumped and his eyes on the table. Laurie swallowed, although she hadn't taken a bite. "I was thinkin' we'd meet them there next weekend, if you didn't have anything planned for then," she continued. "It'd be nice to get out, and spend some time with our friends. Don't you think so, sweetheart? See Barb and Jim again?"

But Mitch didn't respond. He rarely did, these days. When, on occasion, something came out, it was always just that: a response. It was like there was something between his ears and his brain, some kind of snare that caught and entangled her words, and held them so that they would never reach his brain and disturb anything there. Laurie looked at Mitch a moment longer, as if her stare could reach into his head and turn him back on. Then she took in a sharp breath, suppressing anything stronger that might have come out of her, and took another bite of food. They finished the rest of the meal in silence, although Laurie didn't really eat much. Mitch cleared his plate, but didn't seem to know what to do after that. Laurie cleaned the dishes while he just sat at the table. When she was done, she led him away from the table toward the living room. In the hall, Mitch mumbled something. Laurie stopped and peered at him. "Mitch, honey, what did you say? I didn't hear you."

"My finger," he said, looking at his hand. "It ain't there."

Laurie followed his gaze down to his hand, which she held as she led him. His ring finger was missing. There wasn't even so much as a drop of blood where the finger should have been. Just a smooth nub. It was as if it had never been there at all. "Oh baby, what did you do to yourself?" she said, her voice cracking slightly. Laurie looked around on the ground for a moment, but didn't see anything. "You just stay here a moment, okay, and let me see if I can find it. Just stay right here, honey, I'll be right back." She left Mitch in the hall and hurried back to the kitchen. His finger lay on the kitchen table, near where Mitch had been sitting. Laurie picked it up gingerly; again, no blood, like the finger had always been on its own, a separate and solitary thing. She came back to the hallway where Mitch still stood, and took her hand in his. She tried to reattach the finger, but it wouldn't go on. Laurie pushed, she held the finger against the knuckle, but nothing happened. She tried again and again, becoming more and more frantic and upset, but the finger remained separate, and Laurie began to cry softly.

"I'm sorry…" Mitch mumbled, like a child who had made someone sad, and didn't know why. But Laurie only cried more, pushing the finger again and again against his hand. But it remained apart.

*   *   *   *   *

That night, the people of the town all came to see the portal. Mitch and Larry had gone home that afternoon and told their wives about the portal, and what had happened. Then each called his friends and told them about it too, and they all decided to go back up to the hill above the town where the portal stood. Being a small town, news of the arrival of the portal spread like butter on a hot skillet, and soon the area around the portal was crowded with the curious, the bored, and even the wary, who couldn't stay away. Someone had even called one of the nearby city newspapers, but they'd been too busy to send someone out that evening.

Mitch was standing in front of the portal when Samantha Jenkins came over. They'd known each other back in high school, known each other very well. "Heya Mitch," she said.

Mitch turned his gaze to her for a moment. "Hey Sam. How you been?"

"Not too bad," she said, her hands behind her, resting in the back pockets of her jeans.

Mitch remembered the first time they'd met. He'd been so enthralled by her straight, light brown hair. It'd been longer then. Now it was cut around her neck, and her bangs hung playfully down near her chin. "I heard about Ben. Sorry things didn't work out."

Sam shifted her weight to her other foot. "It's okay. I'll get over it. I been dumped before, it ain't the end of the world. I just seem to have a hard time hangin' on to the things I want, that's all."

Mitch looked away from her, not really wanting to meet her gaze anymore. "Yeah, I know," he said. "Sorry 'bout that."

Sam stepped a bit closer to him. "You ain't got nothin' to be sorry about," she said gently. But Mitch's eyes still wouldn't face hers. For a moment, neither said anything. Almost reluctantly, Sam shifted her attention to the portal. Gingerly, she touched her fingers to it, but quickly pulled them back. "Ow!" she said.

"Hot, ain't it?" Mitch grinned at her.

"I heard from Larry that it was hot," she replied. "Jim Jones said so too, and Frank McRae. But Larry said it didn't hurt you to touch it. Said it wasn't hot to you." Sam looked steadily at him. "Is it true?"

Mitch reached up and put his fingers on the portal, and held them there. He looked at Sam, but her eyes were on his hand on the portal. She was fascinated by his hand, and the fact that it could rest on the stone which had burned her so. "I'm the only one, ain't I?" he said finally. Almost reluctantly it seemed, she tore her eyes from his hand and the portal and looked at him. She nodded, and Mitch laughed softly. "Shit. Now that's a little fuckin' scary."

*   *   *   *   *

Laurie woke up sometime in the middle of the night to find herself alone in bed. She got out of bed slowly, and went to the bathroom, but the light wasn't on; she looked in anyway, but Mitch wasn't there. Nor was he in the kitchen, or the living room, or anywhere else in the house. Laurie began to worry. Mitch never went anywhere on his own anymore; she walked him wherever he needed to go. Another search of the house proved fruitless. Laurie ran back to the bedroom, put on her sandals, and grabbed her robe out of the bathroom. She was shaking badly, and had some difficulty getting it on, but managed eventually. On the way out the front door she grabbed her keys and was hurrying down the front walk towards the truck when she heard a voice. She stopped and listened, and heard the voice again. It seemed to be coming from the side of the house. Hesitantly, Laurie moved away from the truck and toward the voice. She noticed for the first time that the moon was whole and in command of the night sky, depriving the night of its shadows. A light mist enveloped the ground, reflecting the moon's light, as if through the ground, the earth's breath was being released into the chilly air. Laurie could feel her feet and legs dragging through the mist as if it was reluctant to let her pass, but had no choice; she didn't care for the feeling, and pulled her robe a bit tighter around her. She rounded the corner of the house and stopped. The mist made it difficult to locate the source of the voice by sight, so she listened. But the voice didn't speak again; instead, Laurie heard a quiet scratching sound, like tiny fingers being raked through the soil. She was about to turn around and head back to the truck, or the safety of the house, which one she hadn't decided yet, when she heard the voice again and knew that it belonged to Mitch. Cautiously, Laurie moved further into the mist, in the direction she'd heard Mitch. The mist had become thicker, and she'd lost sight of the house. She'd lost sight of everything in fact, even her own feet. It was wrapped all around her.

Then she found him. Mitch was on the ground, on all fours, beneath an enormous pine tree. There was something in his hand, but she couldn't make out what it was; he was holding the thing out in front of him tentatively, and speaking gently. "I won't hurt you. It's okay, I promise. It's for you."

Laurie came over and kneeled down next to Mitch, her arm around his shoulder. "Mitch," she whispered. "Mitch, baby, what are you doing out here?"

"He's hungry," Mitch replied, not taking his eyes off the ground in front of him.

Laurie looked at him, and the ground his attention was fixed on, but saw nothing except for the ever-present mist. An uncomfortable feeling was creeping over her. Something didn't feel right. "Who is? Who's hungry?" she asked. "Mitch, there's nothing there."

"Shhh," he said. "You'll scare him away. C'mon boy…you gotta eat…"

Laurie was about to say something when she heard the scratching sound again, and from the mist, in front of Mitch, emerged an armadillo slowly, one little foot at a time. Step by step, it came closer to Mitch, its tiny claws digging into the damp, dark soil and pine needles.

"That a boy," Mitch said. "You don't need to be scared."

The armadillo came up to Mitch's outstretched hand and stopped, sniffing the object Mitch held. Laurie saw that it was a carrot stick, and watched, fascinated, as the armadillo took a few tentative nibbles from the tip. But that was all he took, and the small, grey creature turned away from the carrot, and began to lumber off into the mist. Mitch started to crawl after it. "Come back, you gotta eat…"

Laurie put her arms on his shoulders and held him. "Let it go, Mitch. It doesn't want the carrot," she said. "Let's go in, sweetie."

"But he's hungry," said Mitch, still trying to follow the animal. "I know he's hungry." But the armadillo was gone, and Mitch stopped struggling. Laurie helped him up.

"I know he was, baby," she said gently. "But he's gone. Let him go. It's late, we need to go in." She led him back toward the house. The mist was slowly clearing, and Laurie could see the front lawn and the truck in the driveway.

"I just wanted to feed him," said Mitch. "He was hungry."

"I know," she soothed him, squeezing his hand gently. "It's okay." Laurie led him back into the house and to the bedroom, cleaning the dirt off his bare feet before helping him back into bed. She lay down next to him, and put her arm around his side, holding him as close to herself as she could, hoping to stop his trembling. Sleep came hours later, as the incident replayed itself in her mind again and again. And as she finally slipped exhausted into sleep, a thought drifted into her mind. *Pine trees…there aren't any pine trees in our yard…*

*   *   *   *   *

"Pretty freaky, huh?" Mitch said, grinning at her from the edge of the bed where he sat, naked except for his boxers.

"Yes," said Laurie, looking up from her book. "It's very damn freaky, and I wish you'd quit goin' on about it."

"It's so weird though!" he said as he stood and started bouncing around on the bed. "I can't help it. I mean, where the hell did it come from? Is it even human? What if it came from another world!"

"And here I thought you might finally grow up when you turned 27," she said dryly. Mitch just bounced a bit harder, and continued on to himself. Laurie, finding it quite difficult to read with the bed shaking from Mitch's athletics, decided the book would suit her purposes infinitely better as a projectile, and hurled it at him. It hit Mitch square in the chest, mid-bounce, but didn't faze him. Instead, he bounced over to where she was, plopped down, and straddled her belly.

"Besides, woman," he grinned as he pinned her arms down playfully. "I will talk about whatever I like, and you will listen, because I am a man, and you must respect me, or else you will not get any lovin' from me tonight."

Laurie laughed. "Threats aren't effective, baby, if the person you're threatening isn't going to lose much by ignorin' you."

Mitch looked her dead in the eye, and forced a serious expression to his face. "Woman, I will tie you up if you do not heed me," he said, mustering as much menace into his voice as he could.

She smiled at him. "You promise?"

Mitch grinned and leaned down and kissed her. Laurie pulled her arms free and wrapped them around his neck, pulling him down on top of her. Mitch kissed her cheek, then her chin, and slowly made his way down her neck. Laurie closed her eyes and smiled, delighting in the sensation of his lips softly touching her skin. Mitch leaned back and pulled her t-shirt over her head, exposing her chest.

Laurie opened her eyes. "What a rude young man you are," she said in mock indignation.

"Yup," said Mitch, smiling. "What're you gonna do about it?"

"Move out," she said. "Find me a real man."

Mitch sat up and flexed his muscles. "I'm man enough for ya, babe." Laurie was about to reply when Mitch's stomach gurgled rather loudly, and she instead exploded into a fit of laughter. He looked down at his stomach. "You keep your opinions to yourself," he said, and then turned his attention to Laurie, who was laughing so hard she fell off the bed. "And as for you, woman...I ain't done with you yet!" And with a small jump, he followed her over the side of the bed.

*   *   *   *   *

Laurie sat awake in the dark; a tear fell from her eye and slowly wandered its way down her cheek. She sniffed and wiped it off angrily. Beside her, lay Mitch. He'd been shivering again, worse than before, and it had woken her up. He'd nearly soaked the bed with perspiration. But there was no telltale warmth from his forehead and cheeks to indicate a fever. His skin had been nearly ice-cold, in fact, as was the sweat coming from him. She'd tried to hold him close to share the warmth of her body, and had pulled the thick blanket over them. But the sweating hadn't stopped, nor his shivering; soon it had soaked her shirt and coated her skin, and Laurie had had to let him go. She'd gotten out of bed and made her way to the bathroom, where she had discarded her t-shirt and tried to clean the sweat off of her with a warm washcloth. But no matter how much she'd tried, she couldn't feel clean, and so she'd stepped in the shower and turned the water so hot that it scalded her. That had helped a little. But even as she had crawled back into bed, with a fresh shirt and underwear, the feeling had still been with her, and she didn't sleep the rest of the night.

*   *   *   *   *

Laurie ripped the check out of her checkbook, crumpled it up, and tossed it angrily into the trash bin behind the counter. It was the second one in a row she'd messed up. Her hands no longer had any interest in listening to what her brain was telling them to do, it seemed, and it was really pissing her off.

From behind her, a voice spoke. "Ma'am, I ain't tryin' to be rude, but some of us got other things to do today, if you don't mind."

Laurie spun around and very near slapped the owner of the voice before she realized it was Larry.

"Whoah there, Laurie!" he said, throwing his hands up. "I was just givin' ya a hard time, sweetheart."

"Larry…!" she said, and then took a deep breath. "Jesus, you have got to have the worse fuckin' timing in the world." Laurie took another deep breath. "One of these days you're gonna smartass someone who ain't as quick as I am, and end up with a honey of a welt across your cheek in the shape of a hand, and you'd best believe I'll be rolling on the floor laughing when it happens."

"Okay, okay," he said. "Maybe it wasn't the best timing, I won't argue with you there. But you know if I'd known somethin' was wrong, I wouldn't have given ya any hassle."

Laurie sighed, and tried again to get her check written. "I know, Larry. I'm sorry I blew up. I'm just a little pissed off right now."

151

"Yeah, that I noticed. Normally you at least say hi before you slap me, so I figured somethin' was a bit off. What's got you so riled up?"

Laurie managed to get the check finished without incident this time, and ripped it out of the book with a little too much force, tearing the tip of it off. Bob, the short, grey haired old man who ran the grocery, took the check from her before she could do something really nasty to it. "That'll be jus' fine, Laurie," he said. "I'll make do." Laurie gathered up her bags and headed out of the store, and was loading them into the bed of the truck when Larry caught up with her.

"Well," he said. "You gonna enlighten me, or do I have to start guessin'?"

Laurie tossed another sack of groceries over the side. "Just husband and wife stuff, Larry."

"That's my favorite sort of stuff," he said. "Spill."

She sighed. "Mitch wasn't in bed when I went to sleep last night, and he wasn't there when I woke up this mornin'. I ain't seen him since dinner last night."

"Yeah," Larry said. "I know."

Laurie stopped what she was doing and looked at Larry, but he was looking at his feet. "I was hopin' that wasn't what you was pissed at."

"Well, Larry, you want to tell me just where the hell he was then?"

Larry's eyes still wouldn't meet hers; he started to say something, but didn't seem able to get it out. "He…he was out with…"

Laurie's eyes grew wide, and her jaw fell open a bit. "Oh Jesus, Larry, tell me this doesn't have anything to do with Sam…"

"Aw, shit Laurie," he said, almost ashamed. "Naw, it ain't got nothin' to do with her. I'm sorry, I didn't mean to make you think that."

Laurie let out a breath that she'd been keenly aware she'd been holding. "Well dammit then, Larry, where…" Her voice trailed off.

Larry's eyes finally met hers, and he nodded. "He spent the whole night out at that big stone thing. Told me about it this morning at work." She was quiet a moment. Larry tried to guess what she was thinking, but he wasn't sure what to make of her mood.

"And just what the hell was he doing out there?" she asked finally.

Larry looked away from Laurie at the store window. "He said he was talkin'."

Laurie was a bit perplexed. "With who, Larry?" she persisted.

"I don't know," Larry said. "That's just the thing. When I'd asked if anyone else had been up there, he told me no one else had been around." Larry stopped for a moment and looked away from her before he went on. "He said: 'Not a soul.'"

*　*　*　*　*

Laurie held Mitch as his body shook yet again. It was all she could do now. She didn't know if it helped, but it was something. Laurie was certain she wasn't going to make things any worse. He wasn't sweating tonight, and she tried to take some comfort in that. Finally the shivers subsided, and Mitch's breathing slowly returned to normal. When she was sure he was finished (at least for the time being), Laurie got up and went to the bathroom. She came back out when she'd finished, and stopped for a moment in the dark to look at Mitch. He was lying on his side, just as she'd left him, and Laurie couldn't make out his face in the shadows. Then she slowly moved towards him, and slid into bed next to him, her face to his. She pulled off her t-shirt and dropped it to the ground next to the bed; she had nothing on beneath. Her hands moved to her hips next, and Laurie removed her underwear, discarding them next to her shirt. She lifted Mitch's arm off the bed and slid underneath it so that her body was against his. Pulling herself gently against him, she let her breasts rest on his chest, and entwined her legs with his. Once, then again, she kissed him, letting her lips move across his; but Mitch didn't respond. She kissed him harder, forcing his lips apart with hers, pushing her tongue into his mouth, searching for his. Laurie ran her hand gently along his leg. "Please baby," she whispered to him. "Please, you can do this. For me, baby. I need you, I need you back here with me."
Mitch mumbled something, but Laurie didn't hear it. "What?" she whispered.

"I'm sorry…" he said, almost whispering.

Laurie choked back a sob of relief, and pulled him tight against her. "No, baby, it's okay. You don't have to be sorry. It's okay, you didn't do anything wrong. You're here, thank God, you're here, that's all I want."

"I'm sorry," Mitch whispered again. "I just wanted to feed him. He was hungry."

Again, Laurie tried to hold the back her tears as the hurt and anguish returned, burning stronger than before, trying to consume her. But this time, the tears came anyway.

*　*　*　*　*

Mitch was sitting by the portal when Laurie drove up. The daylight was fading slowly, and twilight making its claim on the evening sky. She put the truck in park, got out, and walked over to where he sat, the light breeze making a mess of his short, light brown hair. He didn't even seem to notice that she'd arrived.

"Mitch."

He turned and looked up at her. "Laurie!" He seemed genuinely surprised that she was there. "Hey babe. What're you doin' here?" Mitch reached up, took her hand in his, and pulled her down so that she sat cradled in his lap, giving her a quick kiss on her head. "It's late. You oughta be at home."

"Just like you," Laurie replied. "But instead I'm here, because you weren't there."

Mitch kissed her forehead again. "I'm sorry, sweetheart. I just came up to take a look at somethin', that's all. Just lost track of time. I didn't mean to keep you waiting. Forgive me?"

"No."

"Aw, c'mon. I'll be good. Won't misbehave again, I promise."

Laurie thought it over a long moment. "Alright. But only if you come home with me. Right now."

"Yes ma'am." Mitch smiled, put his arms around her, and rocked her gently back and forth. They sat like that for a few minutes, enjoying the cool of the evening air and the soft, deep colors that soaked the twilight clouds. Finally, Laurie turned her gaze up to Mitch's face, but his was fixed again on the portal. "It's beautiful, isn't it?" he said.

Laurie disengaged herself from Mitch and got up. "C'mon," she said. "Let's go."

Mitch looked up at her. "Aw, Laurie, c'mon, just a few minutes more. Then we'll-"

"Now, Mitch. I want to go."

Mitch got up slowly and dusted the sand off his jeans. "Alright, then. I'll follow you."

Laurie walked back to her truck, and Mitch to his. She swung the door open and stepped one foot inside, and looked over toward Mitch. He was standing by his truck, one hand on the handle, the door still closed, looking back at the portal. Not just looking at it either. There was something more, she knew it. "Mitch," she called out. He broke off his gaze and looked over to her. "Let's go. And you lead. I'll follow."

"Alright, alright. I'm goin'," Mitch said, and opened the door to his truck.

*　　*　　*　　*　　*

She was on her way out the door, grabbing for her keys, when she noticed they weren't hanging on the key rack by the door. Laurie looked about the floor for them, but they weren't there. It didn't make sense; she always put her keys on the rack, it was pure habit.

Laurie went to the kitchen and started searching for them. She looked under magazines, in the drawers by the sink, beneath the kitchen table, but couldn't find them. She checked the bedroom and the bathroom as well, but couldn't locate the keys anywhere. Again, Laurie tried the kitchen, and having no luck there, went to the living room. Mitch sat silently in the recliner that faced the television. On the screen, Michael J. Fox looked on in shock as his family disappeared from the photo he held, and then his own hand began to follow suit. But Laurie knew Mitch only saw the television set, not the program it was showing. It couldn't show him anything.

She continued to look for her keys, but they didn't seem to be in the living room either. In frustration, she left the room quickly, and tripped, falling hard to the linoleum floor of the hallway. Laurie cursed as she sat up. Her purse, which she'd been holding in her hand instead of wearing it on her shoulder, had become wedged in the legs of a corner table by the doorway, and had caused her fall. She reached over to dislodge it, when she saw a strange shaped object lying beneath the corner table, just behind her purse. Laurie reached instead past her purse and picked up the object, pulling it out from underneath the table to get a better look. She took in a sharp breath when she realized it was an ear. Looking over at Mitch, her fears were realized: the left side of his head was flat. Just hair, and smooth skin where the ear should have been.

Laurie got up from the floor and walked over to Mitch. She crouched down next to him and looked the side of his head. Mitch just sat there, still staring at the television. For a long moment, Laurie remained there by him. "Mitch, honey," she whispered. "Do you want me to turn it up a bit? Would that help?" She laughed. It was a short, sad sound. Then she stood up, ran her hand through his hair once, kissed him gently on the head, and headed back to the kitchen, picking up her purse on the way. Laurie put the ear on the kitchen table and headed to the front door. She grabbed Mitch's keys from the rack, and left the house.

*   *   *   *   *

"Hello?"

"Laurie? It's Larry."

"Hold on a sec." Laurie shifted the phone to her other shoulder, picked the mixing bowl up off the table, and resumed stirring the contents. "Hey Larry. How are ya?"

"I'm just fine, Laurie," he said. "Quick question for you, then I'll let ya go. Is Mitch sick?"

"If you ignore his fondness for farm animals," she replied, "I'd say he's reasonably stable."

"Not that sort, smartass. I meant has he been physically ill lately?"

"He was fine this mornin'," she said. "Why, he throw up at the plant?"

"No," Larry replied. "That's why I'm callin'. We ain't seen Mitch all mornin'. Alan asked me to give you a call to make sure he was okay."

Laurie put the mixing bowl down and picked the phone up. "He left here just like he does every morning, Larry, 7:30am. You mean he hasn't been in at all?"

"No one's seen him. Normally he calls if something's up, so we were at a bit of a loss."

"Maybe he went into Phoenix to pick up something," she offered.

"Doubt it," Larry said. "Toby went in on Tuesday and got everything we needed."

Laurie thought for a moment. "Well Larry, I don't know what to tell you then. You try paging him?"

"Naw, I ain't got the number."

"It's 468…shit, hold on, Larry, I can't remember the rest of it off the top of my head." Laurie reached over to the drawer next to the sink and pulled it open. She fished around a moment, then pulled out a large white index card. She ran down the list of numbers on the card till she found the one she was after. "468-1220."

Larry repeated the number back to her. "Thanks. I'll give it a try. If he calls there anytime soon, check and make sure he got the page, will you?"

"Yeah, no problem. Talk to you later."

"Bye."

The line clicked, and there was nothing but the dialtone. Laurie held the phone to her shoulder for a minute, thinking. Then she put the phone down on the counter, went to the kitchen closet, and pulled out the phone book. She picked the phone back up, cradled it in her shoulder again, and flipped through the book till she found what she wanted. Depressing the button to hang up the phone, Laurie dialed and waited.

Someone picked after the fourth ring. "Roadhouse Ribs, this is Billy,"

"Hey Billy," Laurie said. "It's Laurie.

"Heya Laurie. You all right? You sound a bit rough."

"I'm fine," she lied. "Just my throat. Has Mitch come by today?"

* * * * *

It was dark out. Lately, it seemed like it was always dark out to Laurie. She could barely remember the days anymore. Just the nights, and the dark.

Laurie got out of the truck and walked toward the portal. Her eyes were slow in adjusting to the dark, but she found it anyway; she knew exactly where it was. It had been warm that day, but the temperature had dropped quickly without the aid sun, and the wind was picking up, leaving Laurie uncomfortably cold in only a t-shirt, jeans, and sandals. But despite the discomfort of the cool air on her bare arms, she didn't turn back. Laurie walked up to the portal and stood her ground silently, wilfully, as if through her suffering, her mere presence, she could accuse and condemn it, and the portal would crumble and wither away in the wind. "You give him back to me," she whispered, or perhaps pleaded. "I won't leave till you give him back."

Nothing. Laurie fought, trying to contain the anger that burned and scarred inside her. "Give him back, you give him back!" she cried out, sinking to her knees, her whole body trembling as she struggled for control. "You can't need him, give him back," she whispered, her voice breaking with pain, warm tears almost burning her cheek in the cold air. "Please, what did you do to him? Let him go, don't hold him like this, please. Don't do this. Don't do this to me."

But the portal remained infuriatingly silent.

* * * * *

Mitch stood before the portal. The sun had just made its escape, slipping beneath the skyline, yielding the sky to the stars and the young moon. Mitch touched his hand gently to the portal and ran it slowly down the surface of the stone. It felt warm to him, inviting, the way a chair that's been set near a burning fire does when you're cold. "Are you sure?" he whispered. "You don't mind?" He smiled in delight. "Okay, then. If you're sure."

Mitch lifted his hand from the side of the portal and placed it on the front, inside the center of the sunburst pattern. Gently, he applied pressure, and felt his fingers slide into the stone. For a moment, Mitch let them remain there, submerged just beneath the surface. Then, taking a breath, he slowly pushed them all the way in. Mitch couldn't be sure, but it seemed to be getting lighter out, which didn't make much sense to him, since the sun had just set. Still, Mitch slid his other hand into the portal, and gently started to pull away from the other hand. The sharp edges of the sunburst slowly softened and stretched as Mitch widened the opening his hands were creating. It was definitely getting lighter out now, and Mitch realized why. The portal itself was glowing. And the more he pulled it open, the larger he made the gap, the more intense the light became. Mitch pulled the opening even farther apart; it was over three feet long now, and almost a foot wide. Through his feet, Mitch was sure he could feel the ground trembling. The surface of the portal was radiating now, a bright, piercing white light. The light was coming from everywhere, except for the gap in the center, the opening Mitch had created. As if to be the antithesis of the brightness and intensity of the light, the opening was dark, black. Inside was darker than anything Mitch had ever seen, almost as if any light that dared try to exist near there was swallowed and lost forever.

"Wait..." he started, but to no effect. The opening grew wider now by its own accord, and Mitch was pulled inside.

*   *   *   *   *

Laurie sat cross-legged in front of the portal. She'd been quiet now for some time, just sitting there. Her eyes were still red from the tears, which came in fits and starts. Laurie didn't bother stopping them anymore. She didn't really see the point. In fact, Laurie realized, she didn't really see the point to any of it anymore. There were no more options left to her. She'd tried everything conceivable to her, and they had all failed. She had failed. And now, there wasn't anything more for her to do, except go home. Laurie stood up, and cast a final look at the portal, and turned to leave.

*   *   *   *   *

The hill where the portal lay was dark, and utterly still. There was no sound, no wind, no creatures moving about in the middle of the night. It was as if the entire area had become hollow.

There was no noise as the portal opened back up. From the center of the sunburst pattern, the opening appeared and expanded. The white light flared again, filling the night for a brief moment, as Mitch's lifeless body fell from the portal to the ground where it lay inert, an inanimate pile of arms and legs. Then the portal closed, and silence was restored. The stillness was broken only by the thin wisps of smoke coming from Mitch's skin and clothes, which quickly evaporated in the chilly air.

For a while, Mitch lay unmoving. Then, slowly, he began to stir. One hand at a time, shaking and unsteady, he managed to lift himself off the ground till he was on all fours, but was unable to rise any further. Mitch half-crawled, half-stumbled forward a step. His head hung down between his arms, as if he was so wasted and devoid of strength that he couldn't even muster the energy to raise it. Mitch tried to crawl further, but he instead collapsed to the ground, his breath coming in short, ragged gasps.

"Laurie..." he choked out as he lay there, unmoving, his voice barely even a whisper. "I saw it Laurie." Involuntarily, he swallowed, searching for breath before he continued. "It was so...so..." Mitch's eyelids fluttered briefly, then closed.

*   *   *   *   *

As she turned to leave, Laurie stopped, and then turned back to face the portal. She gazed at it, trying to figure out what it was that had compelled her to turn and stay. But, as before, the portal offered her no answers. Laurie took a deep breath, and let her head hang for just a moment. Then, gathering herself, Laurie walked up to the portal. "I..." she started, as she lay a hand on the center of the portal. But the words she wanted to say wouldn't come to her, and so, instead, she simply whispered: "Goodbye." Then, slowly, the tips of her fingers slid into the portal.

*   *   *   *   *

He found her shortly before daybreak. They lay there together in front of the portal, Mitch holding her tightly in his arms, cradling her motionless body as he rocked her back and forth gently. Mitch could feel the warmth still emanating from her skin and clothes. He cried softly as he ran a hand gently through her hair. "Why, Laurie? You stupid girl, why'd you do it? Why...?"

"Mitch," she whispered, her eyes drifting up to his. "I saw it, Mitch..."

"It's okay, Laurie," he said soothingly. "Shhhh, it's okay."

"I saw it," she went on, her voice almost inaudible. "I saw it, Mitch...it...it-"

"Shush, you be quiet now, everything's going to be okay, you hear me? It'll be okay..."

Laurie's eyes blinked once, again, then fluttered closed. "It was so beautiful..."

"I know baby," he whispered to her, his voice cracking. Mitch held her tightly against his chest, tears burning his cheeks, and rested his head on hers. "Shhhh. I know."

The Maltese Garage Sale
By Stephen Sanders
©2009

It was the kind of day that his mom would have called "plain jane." It was not too hot and not too cool. The sun was shining but there were also a few clouds in the sky. It wasn't the blazing sun of a Central Texas August, when it felt like the air was burning the hair off your arms when the wind blew, and it wasn't the arctic sun of a Central Texas February when it felt like the gusts were freezing your lips off your face when the wind blew.

It was a "plain jane" day.

Greg Carlson sat in the fast food restaurant on Cherry Lane eating the last of his lunch of tacos and soda, reading a passable horror novel about Native American spirits and missing children. Greg's wife, Carol, told people that she could never understand how Greg could read those damn things while he was eating but he seemed to gobble up the tales of blood, gore, ghosts and demons with whatever food he was ingesting.

Greg was a voracious reader – he always had two or three books going at the same time. Horror, yes, but mysteries, historical fiction, historical nonfiction, you name it; Greg could probably have kept a medium sized used bookstore in business all by himself. Once, Carol had asked him if he read so much because he enjoyed it or did she just bore him?

*   *   *   *   *

"Honey," Greg had said smiling, "*You* do not bore me. Life doesn't bore me . . . at least all the time. It just seems like nothing exciting ever happens to me and I like escaping into some of these other places, even if it's the past."

"Well, would you like to do more exciting things?" Carol asked. "We could try and travel more or join a club or something. I always thought that not having kids would free us up to do things like that but maybe it just meant that we got boring. Without kids to worry about, we could travel more, you know?"

"Oh, no! I travel enough working out at the Bomber Plant!" Craig worked for one of the largest defense contractors in the world. "I don't mind doing things but I do NOT want it to involve my ass on a plane any more than I already am!"

161

"What about getting a travel trailer? Or even a motor home?"

"Now you're talking," answered Greg, "Let's get out this weekend and see what there is on the market."

*   *   *   *   *

But that discussion had ended pretty much the way they all did – Greg was always too busy at his job to take time out to try and find a more exciting life and Carol let the subject go because, as a commercial insurance agent, she never had any spare time either. They both meshed back into their daily grinds like the sliding lock on top of a plastic bag, forgetting how exciting they both wanted their lives to be.

Greg finished up his lunch, crumpled the wrappers and carried them on his tray to the garbage can. He started to dump the entire contents of the tray into the receptacle and then realized that he still had half of his soft drink left. He took the plastic cup of soda in one hand, dumped the tray with the other, and then set the tray down in the area demarcated by the plastic railings. Sipping his soda through the straw sticking out of the plastic top, Greg walked out the door to get into his car and return to his "plain jane" day.

Heading back up Cherry Lane, in the direction of the plant and his office, Greg noticed a cardboard sign emblazoned with the words "Garage Sale" on the side of the road. It was one of the countless signs that people staple to telephone poles or trees or stick in the ground on their skinny, metal legs to entice travelers to home-made bazaars featuring junk that the owners no longer need.

"One man's trash is another man's treasure," Greg said under his breath as he passed the sign.

Glancing at his watch, Greg realized that he had thirty minutes before he had to be back and, it's true, you never know what you're going to find at one of those sales. Hardly thinking, Greg signaled a left turn, looked over his shoulder to check the traffic, and turned down a side street, intent on finding his way to the advertised sale.

He found a couple more signs, all in the same colors and marked with the address he had seen on the Cherry Lane sign and easily navigated to the front of a medium-sized, one story, brick and siding house. This was obviously the place because there were assorted pieces of tired-looking furniture sitting along the driveway, piles of clothes here and there, and tables full of knick-knacks. Also, walking among the merchandise, still making adjustments to her amateur merchandising displays, was a twenty-something woman in blue jeans and a white t-shirt.

Greg parked the car and turned off the engine. The trip from the fast food place to the garage sale hadn't been a long one and the air conditioning in the car hadn't really cooled the interior down. The pleasant warmth in the enclosed space, conspiring with the silence that ensued after he turned off the engine, brought on a quick surge of drowsy contentment and Greg leaned back in his seat, stretching and yawning.

As he opened the door, he noticed that the young lady, who had turned and smiled in his direction, was definitely a stunner. She hadn't looked that good from the car but the closer he got the more beautiful she appeared. Her hair was dark brown, almost black, and she had a terrific smile. Her figure, even in the t-shirt and jeans, was beyond impressive – "centerfold quality", as he and his high school buds would have said. Her butt was perfectly sculpted in her jeans, she had a slim waist, the perfect place for your hand while you danced with her or kissed her or escorted her into the bedroom, and her breasts were, even in what appeared to be a man's white undershirt, gorgeous. And, to Greg's male embarrassment, she appeared to be braless and "overly excited" about the prospects of a day spent peddling junk off her driveway.

Her nipples and the dark skin surrounding them were very apparent through the light t-shirt and Greg had a hard time not staring as he walked up the driveway. The woman turned and waved, starting her breasts moving pleasingly.

Greg was a little surprised at her reaction until she spoke:

"You're my first customer!" she said with a smile. Her voice was pleasant with just a hint of an accent; somewhere south of the Mason-Dixon Line, Greg imagined.

"Excellent! I was headed back to work and I saw your sign. I just stopped by on a whim." She had met him about halfway down the driveway and took his hand for a shake. Her hand was soft and warm and she had incredible green eyes.

"Good grief!" thought Greg, "She is freaking gorgeous!"

"Well, you have the pick of the merchandise," said this vision of womanhood, "I wasn't sure when to set up so I just got everything out."

Greg reluctantly let go of her hand. She turned away from him, talking, and as she moved up the driveway Greg's eyes were riveted to the hypnotic motion of her exquisitely shaped ass in her jeans. He could tell that the jeans were old and smooth and would be warm to the touch.

"Damn," he thought to himself, "You're reacting like some school kid. She makes me feel like a school kid! I wonder if she's married? Who cares? I can still fantasize can't I?"

"Where you looking for anything special," the woman asked? Her questions brought Greg out of the argument he was having with himself in his head.

"No; like I said, I just stopped on a whim. I know what my wife would be looking for," there, it was out there, he had a wife, "She always asks if you have any beads. The stuff people make jewelry out of? It's a hobby of hers."

The woman turned back to him, switched on that naturally beautiful smile, and said, "Well, mister, it just might be your lucky day! My mom used to own a part-time beading business and I have more than I'll bet you want to buy."

As she was talking, the young woman turned away, bent over, giving Greg a view of her butt that actually made his mouth begin to water and his crotch to experience a slight stir. She rose up, pulling a box from beneath one of the tables. Setting the box down on a collection of old shoes, the woman stepped back, held out her hands like a show girl and said, "There you go! Let me know if you see anything you want."

Greg smiled. The young lady was either joking with him, knew exactly what she was doing, or was one of those completely naïve beauties that you read about in the letters section of men's magazines.

"Maybe this will be my chance to live out one of those men's magazine letters," Greg thought to himself. "Can you imagine getting some of that? Can you imagine . . .?"

It was difficult to tell what she was thinking because she was acting so naturally. But, she sure was taking advantage of every chance to show him what she had: bending over had pulled her jeans tightly against her most private parts, giving Greg a glimpse of the possibilities that lay beneath her velvety-smooth jeans. The position of her arms amplified the shape and fullness of her breasts and her lovely smile, emerald green eyes, and beautiful face created an image of sensuality and womanliness that would have swayed any man to do this young woman's bidding. She put her hands on her hips, smiled an even bigger smile, and turned away to make some more minor changes to the garage sale.

Greg walked up to the table, still looking out of the corner of his eye at her as she moved about the sale items, and began looking through the items in the box. As he sifted through the stuff in the box he realized that any other time he would probably be intimidated by this display of raw sexiness he was being given. Like most guys, even though they would never in a million years admit it, having a gorgeous, sexy woman acting so friendly and within reach normally made Greg feel uncomfortable, embarrassed and even defensive. There's a reason they're called "stunners."

But, for whatever reason, this woman's friendly, natural demeanor put Greg completely at ease. It was like he already knew her; like seeing her stiff nipples pressed against her thin t-shirt was the most natural thing in the world and something she wasn't embarrassed about in the slightest. So there was no reason he should be embarrassed.

Greg just decided to enjoy the moment and he started going through the beads in the box. Whenever he could, he glanced over at the woman and watched as she bent over or flexed her muscles or leaned over, giving him peeks inside her t-shirt. Going through the box, he immediately knew he had found a gold mine. He knew nothing about beads or the types of things they were made of but the variety of colors alone told him that he was about to make big points with Carol. If the price was right.

Blue, green, pink, violet, black, white, silver, gold, red, orange, maroon, several shades of brown, and some of the beads were multicolored or looked like natural stones. There were strands and strands of them, most on plain white string but others on fishing line or some kind of nylon string.

"How much do you want for these," Greg asked looking up.

The young woman had been folding clothes and she said over her shoulder, not even glancing back, "That's a bunch of stuff that we found in Mom's things after she passed away. I have no idea what they even are so I was just going to charge ten cents per string just to get rid of 'em. Is that too much?"

"Actually," said Greg, "That's probably way too little. I'm like you, I have no idea what some of these things are, but I know my wife pays a lot more than that for beads that look a lot like what you've got here."

As he was talking, the young woman had come back over to stand next to him and look down at the beads. She seemed to be standing very close to him. She was a little shorter than he was so the top of her head was just about level with his nose. The smell of her hair, strawberries, maybe, filled his head and made him think of her in the shower, lathering up her hair. Her breast, soft and full, pressed lightly against his arm. It was an accident, it had to be.

"Well, I can't do anything with them," she said, softly, "Somebody ought to get some pleasure out of them."

Greg could feel subtle movement within his slacks. He was actually getting the beginnings of an erection. He quickly stepped away, looking frantically around the driveway, trying to spy something that would give him an excuse for his sudden movement.

"Wow, this is really pretty! What is it?"

Greg had spied a long garment of dark blue silk that had some kind of hood attached to it. The hood was stiff, almost like a bonnet. It looked like it had been a very expensive garment at one time but that it had now acquired some "character" with age. It was still a beautiful piece of fabric.

"Oh, you like that? My grandmother would have called it a *għonnella*, but I grew up calling it a *faldetta*. My family is originally from Malta and the women over there wear these all the time. It's kind of a hooded cloak and you can wear it different ways."

The woman took the garment from Greg, their hands touching inadvertently as she did so. She slipped the long part of the *faldetta* around her and pulled the hood up over her head. Greg could now see that there was something in the hood that made it billow out, giving it a broad rounded opening which framed the young woman's face perfectly. She pulled the cloak tightly around her body with her right hand and the overall impression was even sexier as a result of the mysterious, alluring quality of the *faldetta*.

"Wow, that's kind of a striking look," said Greg, imagining her naked beneath the folds of the cloak, "The fabric looks so soft and it fits you just right."

She turned on that incredible smile again. It was then that she gave him the look. It was all in her eyes and her lips, the way she was smiling at him. But he suddenly knew that she could tell that he was imaging her nude beneath the cape; that he was thinking about her tumbling on the grass with him. And she was thinking the same thing.

"Here," she said slipping off the Maltese cloak, "Take it home to your wife. It's a gift from me to her and . . . from me to you."

"Oh, I couldn't . . .," started Greg, but as she pressed the silky garment into his hands, touching his hand gently with her fingernails, her fingers, he knew that he would be taking it with him.

There was a moment; and then it passed.

"Hey," she said, "You're going to be buying so many beads you are going to more than make up for whatever I could get for this old thing."

"Okay," Greg said after a pause, "But maybe I need to bring my wife back here tomorrow. We might buy you out!"

At the mention of coming back, which suggested that he would soon leave, a cloud passed over the woman's face. The look of disappointment was clear but the young woman did her best to hide it.

"Don't you want to pick out a few of the strands? That way she'll know what she has waiting for her here."

"Okay. That sounds great. Let me pick out about some now and we can come back tomorrow for the rest or even this evening if you're going to stay open."

The young woman's smile returned as she readily agreed. Greg went to work picking out some of the beads still with no idea what he was choosing. When he clumsily held about thirty of the strands in his hands, he turned to her and said he was ready to pay.

"How many do you have?" she asked.

"Don't you want to count them?"

"No, I trust you," she said with her big smile.

"Well, okay," Greg stammered, "I have thirty here so how much do I owe you?"

"I said ten cents a strand, so that makes three dollars."

"Oh, no," Greg objected, "You've got to charge me more than that! At least a dollar a strand."

"No, no. I told you the price so I can't charge you more."

They bargained for a few more minutes; Greg trying to get the woman to take more money and she, good-naturedly and with a smile on her face, telling him that she wouldn't accept a penny more than the price she had quoted. She flirted with him openly now, even laughingly making a joke that he could "dicker" all he wanted to but she wasn't "going down" on the price.

Finally, they agreed, Greg shaking his head the entire time, and she put the beads into a plastic sack from one of the local supermarkets.

Greg took out his money clip and peeled off a five dollar bill.

"Oh, wait, I haven't even brought out my change bag, yet," Said the young woman, "Come on in for a second so I can give you some change."

She had already started into her garage and, for half a second, Greg thought about just heading off to his car and letting her have the extra two dollars. But, as she turned and smiled from her door, he realized that he might make her mad or embarrassed or whatever and that Carol would be madder than hell when she saw the beads he had and thought about the ones that got away. He headed towards the still open door.

"Damn, son," Greg thought with a grin, "You *must* love your wife; here's this gorgeous babe flirting with you like mad and all you can think about is whether your wife is going to be pissed about the beads. You can think about it all you want; but you know what you're capable of and what you're not capable of."

When Greg reached the door and went in, he realized that he was walking into the young woman's kitchen. At a glance, he could tell that it was modestly furnished but clean. There was a table in the idle of the room surrounded by four chairs and the usual appliances. The only light came through the windows, half-shaded with dark, thick drapes. The edges of the room were dark, unlit, but the center of the room and the sink area was a golden bowl of sunlight.

And then he saw her. She was back near the sink, leaning back against the counter, totally nude.

Some women look so much better in clothes. Even a filmy nightgown can hide the minor blemishes and incongruities that a normal life produces. But this woman, totally, completely, stark naked, was perfect. Her skin, completely devoid of any tan lines, was without blemish of any kind and made Greg think of beaches and cheerleaders and the muscle-taut pelt of a wild cougar prowling the High Sierras.

He had never in his life, never even in his dreams, imagined a woman sexier, more sensuous, more desirable, and his body was reacting accordingly. But, as she lowered her head, peering at him with a much more sensual smile on her lips than the friendly smile she had worn previously, the lips that she was licking as she looked at him with obvious desire, he could only say two words:

"I can't."

Moving slowly, but with the same wild grace of the prowling cougar, she came toward him. She still smiled, smiled as if she knew she would win this argument to, and she said, "You can't? That's a lie. I can tell from your body that you are more than capable of doing everything I want you to do to me."

She looked down at his groin and he followed her gaze. He felt like his pants were stretched out at least a foot in her direction.

"No, no, that's not what I mean," he stuttered, "I mean, I won't. As much as I want to, as much as I am going to regret this later, I mean I won't because I'm married. I could never look my wife in the face again . . . I love her."

She stopped as she reached the small dining table that occupied the center of the room. She leaned back, sitting on the table, opening her legs, her creamy thighs, and slowly stroking the golden, perfect skin that lay between her legs.

"Oh," she chuckled softly, "A slice from a cut loaf is never missed. Just be with me, here, now. Just lay with me and let me give you the gifts that I can give."

As she spoke, the young woman reached up and cupped her perfect breasts, lightly touching her nipples with her index fingers and thumbs.

"Don't you want me? We're all alone. It would be our little secret."

She slid her left hand down the valley that lay between her beautiful tits and her fingers continued downward . . .

"Don't you want this?

"God, yes," Greg said huskily, "You're so beautiful! But even though all of me wants to, I can't, I love my wife!"

Greg closed his eyes and whirled back toward the door, intent on leaving immediately. He dropped the bag of beads. He needed to leave as fast as he could and get in his car and drive away. But the door was closed.

"When did the door . . .?"

That was as far as he got before he was savagely whipped around to face back into the kitchen. The kitchen itself was just like it was before but the woman, if the being in front of him *was* a woman, was very, very different. She was hunched over like some old crone in a fairy tale and she now wore a long, black cape. It covered her completely except for her face. It looked like one of those *faldetta* things and the bonnet-like cowl billowed over what only vaguely resembled a human visage. The skin that showed was gray, at least it looked gray in the dim light of the kitchen, and the eyes were sunk into the thing's head and rimmed with black. Straggly hair covered what he could see of the head and grew out of where a normal human face would have had eyebrows.

But the most hideous change was the mouth. It was less of an oral cavity with lips and teeth and more of a gaping, bloody hole in the middle of the thing's face. As it came closer to him, Greg had the fleeting impression that it was covered over with what looked like a wall of crimson spit. The filmy wetness was translucent and red, like the side of a bubble of blood, and quivering as the woman, or whatever this thing was, moved its head, shifting its gaze from Greg's eyes to his gut to his crotch.

Just before it touched him, just before he passed out in sheer terror, just before he entered a world of blackest black and the deepest abyss, he thought he heard it gurgle:

"Thou art a good man, Gregory Duncan Carlson."

*   *   *   *   *

Greg opened his eyes and he was sitting in his car, the engine idling. He heard a car honking behind him and he looked up to see that the light he had been waiting at had turned green. Years of habit brought his right foot off the break and he gently pressed down on the accelerator. He was headed back to work and, glancing at his watch, he realized he only had nine minutes to be back in his cubicle at the Bomber Plant. He made it with seconds to spare.

*   *   *   *   *

That night, as he sat playing a strategy game on the computer, waiting for his wife to get home so they could make dinner together, he tried to recall what had happened to him at lunch. He had a vague impression of going to a garage sale and meeting someone but he couldn't for the life of him get the memory to come in clear. It was weird.

"I'm getting old," he said out loud. At that moment, he heard the front door opening and the regular sounds of Carol coming in from work. He glanced at the clock on the bottom right hand corner of the computer and saw that she was about forty-five minutes late. That was weird, too.

"Hey, honey! I'm in here!"

After a couple of seconds, Carol came flowing into the room. She was wearing a long, hooded cloak of dark blue silk. The hood was either starched stiff or it had a frame in it because it stood up, much like a bonnet, and Carol's face was framed by the dark fabric giving her a mysterious, alluring look.

"Whoa," he said with a smile, "veerrrry nice!"

As Greg got up and went to take her in his arms and give her a welcoming kiss home, he said, "I love the outfit! Where did you get this?"

"Do you really like it?" asked Carol, breathlessly, "I knew you would! She said you would!"

"Slow down, Mata Hari! What are you talking about?"

"Well, I was coming home from work and I saw a sign for a garage sale and I thought I'd just stop by and see what they had. The old lady that was having the sale was really nice and she showed me a bunch of stuff but what really caught my eye was this cloak. She said it was really old and was from Malta, which is where she was born. It had been her mother's or grandmother's and she didn't want to keep it anymore. She said it made her sad because it made her think of the old days and she'd be happy to part with it. I got it for a dollar!"

"Wow!" Greg said, genuinely astonished, "It's really beautiful! I can't believe that you got it for next to nothing."

"I know! It only cost a dollar but I spent almost an hour sitting there talking to the old lady. She was so proud of her heritage. She wanted to tell me all about these weird legends out of Maltese folklore. Eels that lived in wells and creatures that 'wander the Earth' doing something about spiritual purity.'

"'Spiritual' purity?" asked Greg.

"Yeah, she called them 'gaw gaws' or something like that; bogeymen who could smell out a person's guilt and they'd would follow you around, staring into your eyes. The really icky part was when she talked about their mouths. Kind of grossed me out. But I sure think I made the old lady feel better by letting her go on and on about it."

Greg had picked up the *faldetta* and slipped it over his shoulders, acting the part of an old woman with a gaping, toothless mouth.

In a screechy, old witch's voice, he said to her, "Thank you for listening, deary!"

"Stop it!" Carol said laughing, "You'll ruin the cape!"

Greg looked at his wife, putting on a serious face.

"Thou art a good woman, Carol Rachel Carlson."

The young couple laughed, the *faldetta* was put aside to be dry cleaned another day, and they went in to make dinner, arm-in-arm.

Vagabond

Slowly I rise
Up . . . into the burning blue
Aloft on Tungsten wings

Higher until
With one final effort
I burst the shining bubble
Encasing my native home

I drift with reckless abandon
Reveling in my freedom
With the sure and certain knowledge
Of my strength

But enough of wandering
The time has come
To fulfill the purpose
For which I was conceived

I turn once more
And bid my home
A fond farewell
My family comes with me

And now the voyage begins
My course is set
Had I wanted to
I could not turn back

My name . . . is Vagabond
I am a Starship
And the Universe . . . is mine.

Wendy Easterling
©1990

Echoes of Time

Your voice echoes through my mind,
Reminding me of times gone by.
Gentle times, loving times;
Times that make lovers weep.

Your touch across my skin,
Makes my heart stop then skip several beats.
Heat trailing from fingertips,
Straight to the very core of my being.

Your eyes, so deep and gentle;
Lit from within; your spirit plain before me.
Dark depths spinning and swirling,
Consuming me with their emotions.

Across the miles and years, your presence I feel;
I smell your scent and am comforted.
I long for you but know that we are not meant to be
Not yet … not now … not this life.

My name whispers upon the evening breeze;
Soft and strong … the last thing I hear before I wake …

Across time's touch, the gentle burr reaches my sleep clouded mind …

"Do ye ken hou fyne ya aire tae me, wyfe?"

Kittye Williams
©2009

174

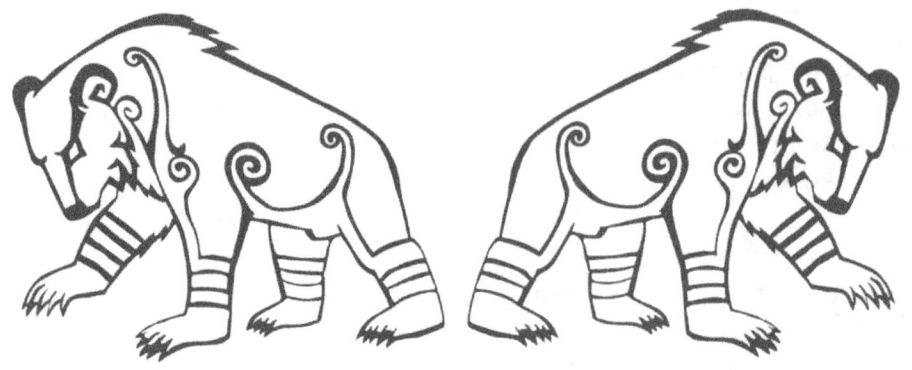

THE TREE IN THE ANCIENT WOODS
By Pamala A. Williams
©2009

The full moon shone occasionally through the building storm clouds over the ancient woods. Jason's footsteps echoed through the silent night as he hurried home from the party. He was late, and knew he'd be in trouble if his parents got home before him.

The party had been a mistake. He wasn't supposed to have gone. His parents had left him watching television and expected him to be there when they returned.

Rushing through the dark, he tripped on some exposed tree roots and fell. Lightning flashed and illuminated the area. Jason saw an old crumpled shoe box in a hollow in a near-by tree.

He reached into the hollow and brought out the shoe box. Carefully lifting the lid, he peered inside. He found an old candle that was almost used up, a strange-looking ring, and a fragile roll of parchment.

Unrolling the parchment, he read the words in the lightning flashes:

"A full moon wish upon this ring

And ancient magic will take wing.

But of the wish there must be care

To wish for only what you dare.

A word misspoken any there be

Could turn a man into a tree."

"Maybe I could wish I were home," Jason thought.

Then he heard the whisper. It said, "Give me back my treasure."

Jason looked around for the source of the voice. The lightning flashed. It was then that he noticed the tree. The tree had a pair of eyes. Sad, haunting eyes. The bark below they eyes almost looked like a mouth in a permanent "o". Low, bare branches almost looked like arms with twisted fingers on the ends.

"Give me back my treasure," whispered the voice again.

Jason, his heart pounding, placed the parchment back into the old shoe box and carefully replaced the lid. He slid the box back into the hollow. The eyes of the tree closed to reveal only bark.

As lightning flashed again and thunder rumbled in the distance, Jason ran home, willing to take any punishment his parents were prepared to extend. He silently hoped he would never end up like the tree in the ancient woods.

Tempelton Black

Tempelton Black, always seemed to have a knack.
Though it is not a fact, it is said, he once was a fine diplomat.
With long braid down his back, no man dare give him flack…
If one did have such a brain of lack, he'd use it, with a swish-crack!

For this most charming chap, finding treasure is a snap.
He needn't even have a map, once one has his special nightcap.
Too late to know of the trap, he or she is taken without mishap.
Head pounding, covered with burlap…in a word, kidnap!

Whether you're young or old, whose beauty has been compared to a marigold,
Noble gentry, men most bold, whom songs as well as stories are told.
 Be assured for a price you will be sold, you who have silver and gold.
Black's heart is stone cold. He will not bend, nor fold.

So . . . if you see a man whose hair, is like the tail of your best mare.
 At your next grand affair, one of your guests might vanish in mid-air!
With a note specifying when and where. Pay, they will return no worse for wear.
Not, then best say a prayer, they can be almost anywhere!

Shana L. Martin
©2008
Inspired by God

The Sacred Flame
By Wendy Easterling
©2009

After meditating for a short while, the Fire Goddess appears with Her Commander, both dressed in resplendent finery fit for the impending occasion. She in red and gold silken brocade; he in leather armor adorned with the plumes of birds-of-prey; each a perfect foil for the other. They proceed to the center of the clearing, looking neither right nor left. When they reach the Fire Circle, they both turn to address those gathering close in anticipation. Lifting up her voice, the Goddess speaks...

"Friends, guests and loyal followers, we gather this night to Celebrate and Consecrate our new Home with Sacred Fire. For those of you who have followed me here, and held me up through pain, suffering and trial by Fire, this is our new beginning, our Journey of Victory!

"Those of you who have pledged loyalty to me, and through me to the Flame, are exalted amongst your peers, and shall find reward in this event, though it be neither asked for nor expected. This is my gift to you . . . and my guests, who are newly become friends. This is my offering to you for your Pilgrimage. May you carry the embers of the Eternal Flame with you on your return Journeys, or be welcome to stay, if you so choose. I would treasure such as all of you in my service, and as my companions!"

"Please, gather close, and witness the Drawing Down of the Sacred Flame!"

The Goddess steps into the Fire Circle, mounting the logs laid like stairs, reaching the pinnacle so that Her feet are level with the heads of the guests who stand well back, watching in anticipation. As She reaches the top, She slowly turns until She has seen each direction of the new Realm, beginning with the direction She came here from, and ending facing the Full Moon.

She raises Her arms, graceful fingers pointing to the stars. Throwing back Her head to expose Her long white throat, She begins to sing, a wordless Paean offered to the very Stars whose Fire spawned Her. A faint glow begins to gather around Her, as though fireflies are drawn to Her heat and wish to offer Her their light in exchange. The glow brightens, and tiny blue-white flames begin to flicker from Her fingertips, spreading slowly with the melody of Her song along the length of Her upraised arms. The argent flames twine down Her sides, encircling Her voluptuous form before continuing the journey to Her delicate feet, poised upon the pyre erected in Her honor and dedicated to Her inner Nature.

She speaks, Her voice slightly deepened with sudden effort...

"I draw this Sacred Fire from its Source in the very Stars of the Universe, from the Sun of this World, and from the Core which it hides and holds! I Offer it to the Night, and the Sky Deities, as Illumination in the Darkness, shining Light on those things which are Hidden, and Unknowable... as Warmth in the late hours, when the Body is weary and vulnerable... and as a counterpoint to the Pulse of Blood through the Veins, which carries the Divine Spark and leads us in the Sacred Dance of Life!"

As She speaks, the Flames begin to grow brighter, and heat pours from Her in waves toward the onlookers and out into the night. By the final word, Her throat is open in an almost primal scream; as if the effort of channeling, controlling and containing the Sacred Flame becomes agonizing Ecstasy! Animal voices echo from the surrounding wood, rising to a cacophony during this speech, before abruptly silencing with the end of the words issuing forth from the Goddess.

As the Goddess ceases speaking, the Flames burst forth from Her skin, devouring Her garments yet marring no part of Her Flesh! She is clothed in Living Flame, leaping and swirling like a caged Beast, as Her breast heaves with the effort of containment and control.

She flicks Her fingers, and suddenly, a single deep Drum beat rolls across the clearing, as the Sacred Fire engulfing the Goddess leaps in response. Another beat, another leap, and suddenly the Beast begins to take notice of the Geas exerted by the slow pulse of the Drum, and howls and struggles against constraint like a crazed Demon under compulsion of Summoning!

The Monk rushes forward to the edge of the Circle and begins a rapid chant, whirling in a clockwise direction, sprinkling pungent herbs and shimmering powders into the edges of the Pyre where the Flame has not yet spread. Suddenly, just as he finishes rounding the circle for the third time and steps back rapidly, the Flames lick at the logs piled under it and in one motion envelop the pyre in a ravening inferno!

As the onlookers watch in stunned and mesmerized fascination, the Goddess begins to rise on the howling wind created by the desperately struggling Flame seeking freedom, and fuel. As She rises, Her body begins to slowly spin, Flaming hair writhing with tendrils reaching for something to grasp, arms out-flung and fingers stretched to near breaking with effort. The movements of Her fingers correspond to the pounding hammer blows of more Drum voices, as a Rhythm starts to take shape, increasing in volume and frequency, until every instrument in the clearing is involved. Wedded into a complex and compulsive Rhythm, the vibration causes the onlookers to step and sway without realizing it, as the Divine Pulse begins to beat within each breast, and shift each foot in time with the rolling thunder of the Drums!

The shimmering Goddess, limned with Sacred Fire throughout Her entire being, moves within the Rhythm of the Drums, and slowly the writhing, screaming Beast conforms to the reverberation echoing through the clearing, first reluctantly, then with dawning enthusiasm, until Goddess and Flame are one, rejoicing in the feel of the Melding, and becoming the Rhythm of Life itself, whole and ecstatic in the joining, Dancing within and without each other, until there is no separation. Two disparate beings become One in Divine Gestalt . . .

During this transformation the onlookers are drawn into the drama, no longer able to merely observe, but become the Rhythm Riders, moving with the transformation as though feeling it themselves, all but the tall, still figure of the Commander of the Sacrifice, whose eyes never leave the Goddess, and who does not retreat from the heat of the Sacred Flame coursing through Her. He knows She will have need of him soon, and he stands ready to lead Her from the pyre, knowing that the heat can never touch him while She exists.

As the Sacred Fire is transformed through the Goddess into a Joyous and playful Partner, no longer ravening Devourer, it begins a complex counterpoint Dance of its own, weaving back and forth to the Drums, creating a red-gold mesh which extends around the bare, Flame-clad Flesh within the Heart of the Pyre, until it has formed itself into fine, flowing raiment, concealing the generous curves so recently kissed only by Sacred Flame. The weave settles itself over breast and along hip and thigh, until She is dressed once again as Goddess, in living Fire made Cloth-of-Gold by the Transformation so recently taken place before the onlookers-turned-revelers.

Gradually the Fiery figure's Dance begins to slow, as the Goddess descends the column of liquid heat she twirls upon, settling onto the now burning tower at the center of the Circle of Dancers, and the Commander steps forward, knowing his role in the unfolding drama, and eager to play his part. He reaches into the Heat and Flame without fear or hesitation, knowing himself safe from the raging conflagration this Goddess/Woman has ridden, and now wears as Eternal, yet ever shifting, silken Armor. As the trance leaves Her, so too, does the supernatural Strength imparted by the Ceremony, and She falters as he reaches out to catch Her falling form in his waiting arms. The Rhythm rumbles on, carrying the oblivious Dancers with it, as Commander carries Goddess, now more mortal woman than at any other time, swiftly to the pavilion, where the sides fall of their own volition and the ties at corners twine themselves tightly together, and lamps alight with the last of the Sacred tendril remaining in the limp form, creating a safe haven where mortal man and momentarily mortal woman regard one another in the dim light of this world apart from the revel spinning swiftly into mindlessness only yards away, yet not even in the same Universe as the two who know no other thought at this moment but each other. There is one final movement to this Sacred Dance, and only these two know the steps . . .

The Passing of the Mantle
By Scott Goodrich
©2009

I remember the first time I saw him. I was walking home from work one day and I had worked late so it was very dark. I was passing a particularly dark alley when I heard some scuffling and something breaking like glass. When I turned and looked down the alley, I saw a large man standing in the middle of the alley about half way down to the next block. I could see clearly, from the light of the large doorway he stood in front of, what had broken. It was a very large chandelier he had been working on. It had come loose from its hanging hook and crashed down onto the cement floor, shattering into a million pieces and breaking the heavy iron work he was creating. He looked white in the light as if he had barely escaped with his life, when from out of the shadow he created behind him there arose a figure clad in an all encompassing robe. He carried a large scythe that stretched about three feet above his head, and he was reaching for the man's shoulder.

The large man turned to see what new horror had beseeched him. The man shifted to one side to avoid the creatures touch, for he knew what he was there for. The large man set about searching for something in the alley to fend off this robed figure which had come for him. Frantically, he found a disconnected power line that was being worked on during the day, and turned off at the pole. The robed figure, moving slowly towards him with an outstretched arm, beckoned to him. When his arm was almost within reach the man thrust the switch up and shot his arm forward with the wire into the breast of the robed figure.

The pyrotechnics were something to behold. The entire alley was lit up like the fourth of July. The robed figure lurched and bobbed like a puppet on its strings, caught up in a hurricane wind. It fell to the ground like a rag doll tossed about carelessly. It landed into a large puddle of water that had collected from an earlier rain fall.

On the ground, apparently stunned senseless, the robed figure reached up to the man standing over him. Breathless after the ordeal, the man seemed to be almost in a trance or dazed. He reached out apologetically to the now clearly skinless hand that reached up to him. Upon grasping the bone hand, there came a serene peaceful look and stature to the man. As he helped the robed figure to its feet, the man leaned in to hear what the figure had to say.

The robed figure spoke for a moment, inaudibly from my position, to the man and then the man stood straight up, turned to face the opposite end of the alley, and began to walk. The robed figure stood watching as the man walked away. As the man got further and further away he began to vanish, slowly, until there was only the robed figure there in the alley and me at the opposite end watching.

I stood there mesmerized by what had just transpired, when the robed figure turned in my direction.

I stood there frozen with fear, caught unaware. The fact that I was at the end of the alley did not matter, when a bone chilling streak went up my spine as in a second the robed figure was standing not half a foot from me. He apparently moved with a thought to where I was. We stood there for a moment or two, the robed figure regarding me with a sense of astonishment.

He finally spoke, and when he did, it was like the sound of the graveyard coming to life. He asked me my name, short and simple. I hesitated for a moment confused as to what I should say. Then, unbidden, my name came forth from my lips, as if he had reached inside of me and pulled it out with his boney hand.

He spoke again for a time telling me that in all the time he had served in his station no one had seen or stayed to witness the end of someone. I stood there still frozen in my body, fearful of what may come. He somehow sensed this and assured me that my time was not yet here.

We stood there at the alley way for what seemed like hours. He talked about many things that he had seen and done throughout his service, and I began to realize that he was lonely for company; you know someone to talk to and not just send off to the other side.

I noticed the passage of time because the sun was starting to come up. Feeling less frozen, and somewhat sorry for him, I finally spoke up and said that I had to get home. He fell silent again. It seemed like I had just stabbed him in the heart. I spoke up quickly, and asked if he would like to accompany me to a nearby coffee shop that I frequented on early mornings after work. He seemed to come "alive" again and expressed a want to do just that.

We walked down the block to the coffee place all the while he regaled me with tales of his exploits throughout his service. Some of which were, if I remembered my history correctly, from the early Roman days. He expressed that in the old days business was good and that he could barely keep up with the demands.

I let out a laugh and he fell silent, then almost at a moment too late he himself burst into laughter, almost falling over we laughed for a good long time. When we gathered our composure we had finally made it to the coffee shop. I held the door open for him as he went in and I followed. The waitress asked me how many, I responded two, and she asked if I was meeting someone.

I turned with a confused look to my new friend and he said that no one else but me could see him. I quickly responded to the waitress that indeed I was meeting someone and apparently they were running late. She seated me, and my friend tagged along and took the opposing seat in the booth she had appointed to me.

We sat there for hours talking back and forth. I can't tell you how many weird and strange looks I got from people around me. After a while I put my ear bug for my phone on and I didn't get so many looks.

His tales were fascinating and mesmerizing and we lost all track of time. It seemed like time had stopped in a way, and that the rest of the world just went away for a while. I had never met anyone so interesting in my life. Around noon I felt we had overstayed our welcome at the shop and conveyed this to my new friend. He spoke up and asked what I wanted to do next. I was caught up in the thrill of everything and said that we should move to the park where people didn't mind you talking to yourself. He gave out a laugh that seemed more like a groaning of an old door. I paid my tab and we left, making our way on towards the park.

When we got to the park he let on how refreshing it was to take a break from his duties to enjoy someone's company. He then went on to tell me that I was a very special person to be able to see him and that that did not happen very often. In fact, very rarely he said. I was enriched by his compliment and felt that we had a sort of kinship, a bond if you will, that transcended everything.

He then went on to explain that I had a choice to make for the future. He explained that all the stories he told me were a history of his duty and that there was even more stretching back to the beginning of time itself. This was his duty also to be a keeper of history as well as the final step for those passing on. I was not sure what I had to do with it and expressed that to him. He got right to the point that he was sure that I was the next appointed in line to assume the mantle that he himself took up from the previous owner.

I said that I was not sure I was ready for such a great task and not sure if I could carry such a huge responsibility. He assured me that when he took up the mantle he himself expressed such concerns, and said that there was a trial period with, "on the job training", that must be gone through to make sure that indeed I was the one. I was still taken aback by the huge responsibility of it all, but thought about it for a moment and it just seemed like the next step in life for me.

I really didn't have any family, or friends. Most of the people I knew were just acquaintances. I realized upon my reflections that I really did not have a lot going on here and I could take it or leave it, so I accepted his offer.

He was pleased and expressed a desire to get things started right away. I was again taken aback by his eagerness and expressed a want to rest till tomorrow and get started then. He gave a chuckle and asked me to touch the scythe he held out for me.

I reached out a nervous hand to grasp the wooden handle and upon making contact with it I was immediately without any tiredness or pain. I felt as if I had slept millennia and had just awoken refreshed. My vision was so clear as I looked about at the people in the park; it was as if I looked into their souls if I concentrated a little.

He said that there was no time to waste because we were not given the luxury of a day off. The world kept on turning and time did not wait for anyone, not even us. He expressed that we should move quickly for we had an appointment waiting for us. The next thing I knew we were in a different part of town, one that I did not recognize, in fact I didn't think we were in the same town at all upon looking around.

He grasped me by my shoulder and we moved closer to a store front where a man had just fallen over grasping his chest in abject pain. People gathered around to render aid to the man but to no avail, he had already passed. I knew this because I saw him standing over his own body looking confused.

He looked about and was heartbroken for what he was leaving behind, a good women of a wife was nearby grieving for her lost love. He knelt at her side and tried to comfort her but he could not. We moved closer to the man as he stood and wept for his life. My friend reached out and touched him on his shoulder and he looked up with relief.

My friend leaned in and whispered to the man and this time I heard every word he uttered. Suffice it to say he was comforting the man and told him in such a way that it was his time to move on and once through the door he pointed at, mere feet from us that had appeared out of nowhere, that things would make better sense to him and that his family and friends would join him before he knew it.

The man, grateful, nodded his acceptance and walked towards and through the door, where there was a bright light shining through. I turned and asked if my friend had ever been through the door. He told me that we were not allowed through the doorway until our service was at an end. I looked at him, knowing that I would be in his place comforting him and pointing him onward to a new beginning very soon.

Time seemed to flow easily as we moved about doing our business. I learned everything, from my new friend, about history and what and how things worked in our line of business. I enjoyed the time we spent together and the long conversations we would have about things.

I grew more and more confident with each passing day, or year, it is hard to keep track. It would seem that I had lost all track of what day or year it was. It came suddenly one day in the afternoon when my friend turned to me and said that it was finally time for him to move on.

I was very confident at this point after all the training and the passing of all of history to my care. He had moved us to Paris under the Eiffel Tower, where he turned to me and handed the Scythe over and began to disrobe. I was shocked when he pulled the remaining part of the robe off. There was not a formless skeleton standing there before me, but a man in his early thirties maybe, nothing special about him really, just an ordinary looking man.

He passed me the robe and bade me to put it on. Upon donning the robe, I was filled with wonder at the sights that I could see all about me. I looked at my friend and I knew it was his time. I started to weep uncontrollably for my friend, he reached out and said that we would meet again soon.

He embraced me and I could not let him go. After a few tense moments he pulled away and I saw that he had been weeping as well. He spoke up for the last time and said to me, "You have been a great friend and I could not have chosen a better replacement, you have done me proud and I shall wait for you when your time comes."

I nodded and spoke to him for the last time, "I will never forget you and I look forward to the times that we shall meet again so that I may pass on my adventures and history the way you have done for me."

I reached up and put a bony hand on his shoulder and pointed with the scythe. He turned and walked towards the door. He paused at the threshold and looked back, gave a wave of his hand and turned back and disappeared through the door. I took a deep breath and for a long moment missed my best friend. I suddenly came to the realization that I was late for an appointment and hurried off to work.